NORTH WEST RAIL TRAILS

Historic Railway Rambles

Gordon Suggitt

Published by Sigma Leisure – an imprint of
Sigma Press, 1 South Oak Lane, Wilmslow, Cheshire SK9 6AR, England.

British Library Cataloguing in Publication Data
A CIP record for this book is available from the British Library.

ISBN: 1-85058-688-8

Typesetting and Design by: Sigma Press, Wilmslow, Cheshire.

Cover photographs, from top left: the Flying Scotsman at Brooksbottom, February 1993; the trackbed of the former Bacup-Rochdale line near Britannia; 'Sir Nigel Gresley' at Ramsbottom, January 1998 *(Jenny Suggitt)*

Maps and photographs: Gordon Suggitt, except where indicated.

Printed by: MFP Design and Print

Foreword

– by Sir William McAlpine, Chairman of the Railway Heritage Trust

The introduction of railways in the nineteenth century had an enormous impact on the population of the British Isles. Industrialists, landowners, urban and rural dwellers witnessed the birth of a new form of transport which revolutionised the way they conducted their lives. The impact of that revolution is still with us today.

The development of the railway network and the accompanying relative ease with which goods and people could be transported long distances has a significant place in our nation's history. Nowhere is that significance greater than in the north west of England.

Not all the early railways have survived by any means. Indeed, it can be argued that many of those actually built or planned could not really be justified and, inevitably, closures of routes or parts of routes have occurred.

Whatever the reasons for closure of parts of the network, the legacy of closed lines has created an opportunity for their rediscovery by walkers. In this book, Gordon Suggitt offers the walker not only easily understood directions to access the former railway routes, but also the opportunity to understand something of their early construction and use.

I welcome his imaginative approach which will ensure that many more walkers will now use these former transport corridors which form such an important part of our history. Not only will they use them, but they will find that the quality and enjoyment of their chosen walks will be greatly enhanced by reference to an exciting publication.

The Hon Sir William McAlpine, Bt

Contents

The Walks

Key to route maps

- ← – – Route of walk
- Route along tarmac
- Route along disused railway
- ······ Disused railway not part of the walk
- Railway in use
- ● Station in use
- Bridge
- PH Public house
- PO Post office
- Church with a tower
- Church with a steeple (spire)
- ✝ Church with neither tower or steeple

Location map

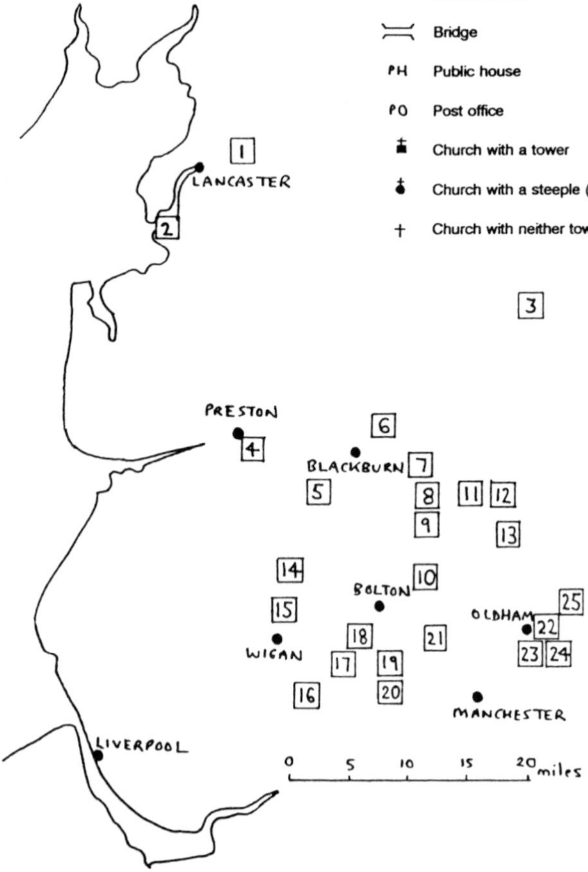

LANCASTER
PRESTON
BLACKBURN
BOLTON
OLDHAM
WIGAN
MANCHESTER
LIVERPOOL

1 2 3 4 5 6 7 8 9 10 11 12 13 14 15 16 17 18 19 20 21 22 23 24 25

0 5 10 15 20 miles

Introduction

The idea for this book came from stumbling across, usually by accident, lengths of disused railway accessible to and walkable by the public. The impression, even amongst walkers, is often that these will be rubbish-filled, weed-choked cuttings in grubby townscapes sealed off by impenetrable barbed wire. However, a surprising number of stretches of former rail line in the north-west are in pleasant surroundings maintained by the local authority or other organizations. These usually have a walkable surface with stiles and gateways, and provide a variety of settings. Yes, there are some lengthy cuttings, but also embankments, bridges, station sites and even a tunnel. What most of them do lack is clear access, often starting in obscure spots such as factory car parks, or even in one case, at a roundabout on the A6. Coupled with this is a lack of sign-posting, so that it is all too easy to drive past these routes without even knowing they exist. Not surprisingly then, in most cases these walks along old railways are only known to local people. This book aims to remedy that by bringing these remnants of our transport history to a wider audience, both locally and at least regionally within north-west England.

I have tried to combine the length of old railway with a different return route to give a circuit of between 2 and 5 miles. These return routes may give views of the railway's setting or follow a different transport link such as a canal or a preserved railway. (The railway is usually first so that a retracing of the route back along the railway is feasible, if preferred.) The length has been kept down as these are meant to be short but informative strolls dealing with the railway and its environs as well as the walks themselves. I have tried for as much variety of routes as possible, in some cases omitting additional walks along the same line. Other potential walks have been left out because they did not lend themselves to a circuit or were in too urban a setting. I have tried to indicate these in the text so that those interested can devise their own strolls. This book does not exhaust the possibilities for walking old railways in the north-west.

Practical Points

These walks are not in high moorland settings. Many of them are in comparatively sheltered locations close to towns and villages. Specialised walking equipment would therefore not normally be required. An exception to this would be footwear, where stout shoes would be a minimum and walking boots or even Wellington boots advisable after wet weather. Old railways, especially in cuttings, can be muddy, as can some of the return routes, for example along canal towpaths. However, these remnants of former railway are usually maintained and impassable stretches have been omitted. In a few cases where the muddiness might be a deterrent, this has been identified in the introduction to the walk. Most of the walks do include some walking along tarmac – this has been kept to a minimum wherever possible. Some stretches are in urban settings – these too have been kept as short as possible but do provide some interesting glimpses of Tyldesley and Oldham, for example.

In almost all cases, the suggested **maps** for the walks are at a scale of 1:25,000. This is because the level of detail is much greater then on the 1:50,000 "Landranger" maps, allowing easier identification of both former railway features and the route round farm buildings etc. The 1:25,000 maps have been for some years mostly issued as the "Pathfinder" series, with some larger "Outdoor Leisure" sheets e.g. "South Pennines". Now the "Pathfinders" are being replaced by "Explorer" maps, still at 1:25,000 but covering a much larger area. This will allow the coverage of the walks by relatively few maps – the "West Pennine Moors" sheet for example includes six of the walks in this book. The one point in favour of the 1:50,000 "Landranger" maps is that they do show most of the walkable old railways in large black dashes, whereas the "Pathfinder" maps in particular did not mark them at all. For that reason, it is still worth referring to the "Landranger" maps which cover the walks as follows:

Sheet 97, "Kendal and Morecambe" – Walk 1

Sheet 102, "Preston and Blackpool" – Walks 2, 4 and 5

Sheet 103, "Blackburn and Burnley" – Walks 3, 5, 6, 7, 8, 11 and 12

Sheet 108, "Liverpool" – Walks 14 and 15 (part)

Sheet 109, "Manchester" – Walks 9, 10, 13, 15 (part), 16, 17, 18, 19, 20, 21, 22, 23, 24, and 25

Public Transport

Information has been confined to an indication of the possibilities available for those wishing to reach the locations of these walks by bus or train. Details of services within Greater Manchester (Walks 10 and 14-25) can be obtained from GMPTE on 0161 228 7811. There doesn't seem to be an equivalent single source of information for services in Lancashire, where the relevant County Information Centres are as follows:

Lancaster (Walks 1 & 2): 01524 841656

Nelson (Walk 3): 01282 698533

Preston (Walk 4): 01772 556618

Chorley (Walk 5): 01257 241693

Accrington (Walks 6 and 7): 01254 872595

Rawtenstall (Walks 8, 9, 11, 12, and 13): 01706 213677

These County Information Offices should be able to provide details of *all* bus and train services within the county – not just their local area. The same applies to the offices in Burnley, Clitheroe, Fleetwood, Leyland, Lytham, Morecambe, Ormskirk and Skelmersdale.

A Note on Railway History

There is no way a book of walks can give a comprehensive history of the railways in an area and that has not been attempted here. Instead, a brief indication of the background to the lines featured in the walks has been provided to add interest. Errors have, hopefully, been avoided but there has been some simplification, especially over the start of the railways in the area between 1828 and 1859. This is because individual lines were usually started by their "own" company, with amalgamations into larger companies often taking place before the line was finished. For example, the East Lancashire Railway was formed from five once-separate companies each responsible for the start of one line. As each of these lines included in this book was part of the ELR by the time it opened, it is the latter company that is credited with the line.

In each walk, the practice shown above has been used, whereby the first reference to a railway's name is given in full, followed by its initials for subsequent mentions. The exception to this is the LNWR which is so widely referred to in this way it seemed pointless to use its full title. It and the other initials used in the text are as follows:

ELR = East Lancashire Railway

LYR = Lancashire and Yorkshire Railway

LNWR = London and North Western Railway

LUR = Lancashire Union Railway

Anyone wishing to take the history of the railways further will find a wealth of books available. The "Bibliography and Further Reading" section gives some possibilities although the list is by no means exhaustive.

Acknowledgements

Many people have offered help and information. I would particularly like to thank staff at Rawtenstall Public Library Local Studies Department, Blackleach Country Park, Walkden Public Library, Bury Planning Department, and Park Bridge Visitor Centre. I would like to acknowledge the use of old photographs from the collections of the late J. Davenport, C. H. A. Townley, J. Peden, J. Ryan and J. A. G. H. Coltas, and thank A. Haynes for his help with copyright. Finally, I thank family and friends for their encouragement with this project.

1. Lune Valley Stroll

Caton to Halton

Almost 9 kilometres (5½ miles) of the former Midland Railway line east of Lancaster have been converted into a path and cycleway. This walk visits two of the station sites, separated by fine river scenery.

Start: Caton station site. GR 531648.

Distance: 6.1km (3¾ miles) on almost completely level terrain, although there is a short sharp climb away from the river on the return journey. The former rail route is paved throughout, but the return north of the river uses tracks and paths which can be wet and muddy.

Map: Outdoor Leisure 41 "Forest of Bowland and Ribblesdale"; alternatively, Pathfinder 637 "Burton-in-Kendal and Caton".

By car: The Lune Valley can be reached from the M6, junction 34 (NE of Lancaster). Take the A683 eastwards, towards Kirkby Lonsdale, to Caton. At the mini-roundabout in the village centre, turn left into Station Road. There is "official" parking along the left of the road. (Note that this is limited to four hours, which should be ample for the walk.)

By public transport: There are regular bus services between Lancaster and Hornby, with some buses continuing to Kirkby Lonsdale and Ingleton. Bus stops are just off the A683, on Brookhouse Road.

The branch from Clapham (North Yorks) to Lancaster and Morecambe was actually opened by the North Western Railway in 1849-50. Despite its name, the company was never associated with the LNWR and to avoid confusion was usually referred to as the "Little" North Western. By 1852 the line was being worked by the Midland Railway, which then leased and later bought the "Little" North Western (1871). The development of Morecambe as a seaside resort and nearby Heysham as a port (1904) gave the line much use by trains from West Yorkshire which continued until closure in 1966. (Services to Morecambe transferred to the Wennington-Carnforth route further north.) The stations at Halton and Lancaster Green

Ayre closed with the branch, the ones at Hornby and Caton having closed in 1957 and 1961 respectively. There had also been short-lived stations at Wray (closed 1850) and Claughton (1853). Considerable remains exist at Caton and Halton stations, as indicated in the walk description, and the trackbed is walkable from Bull Beck (east of Caton) to Lancaster, but most of the route from Caton to Wennington has returned to farming use.

The Walk

From the bus stop or parking space, walk along Station Road to the remains of Caton station. It is the former Station House, now a private residence, that first catches the eye, but across the road, the goods shed now has another use – as a church! Turn left past these buildings and go round the wall to gain the trackbed. This leads alongside the buildings of Caton, including the fine sandstone Thirtell Cottages. These were once mill-workers' homes, a reminder of the area's industrial past. The Caton area alone once had eight mills and plenty of evidence of former industry will also be seen at Halton. Next the line's surroundings are pleasantly wooded as it crosses a lane deep below, before a stretch across fields leads to the first of two rail viaducts over the Lune. This five-span structure gives good views of the stone bridge for the road just downstream, and is itself easily viewed by descending to the riverside at the right of the viaduct's far side. The railway then goes under a road bridge, then over the second, less accessible, viaduct, this time of six spans.

The path continues, first through woodland, then under a modern bridge and through a shallow cutting, before it becomes a track which is the access road for North-West Water's "Lune Intake" from the river. The track gets closer to the river which can be first heard, then seen, tumbling over a modern weir. Now the track narrows and enters a long straight stretch next to the river which flows turbulently over the remains of older weirs. The trackbed begins to bend gently right, passing under power lines, as the buildings of Halton now come into view across the river. After a small sewage works on the left, a gate across the track appears ahead, beyond which is an area of car parking next to the former Halton station. Still standing

At Wennington Junction in 1959, an express heads left on the Carnforth line while a loco waits on the now-disused line to Caton and Halton *(J.A.G.H. Coltas)*

on the north-side platform are the offices and goods shed, in a reasonable state of preservation as they are used by Lancaster University Rowing Club. It is worth going down the path on the right just before the buildings to view their back, with two projecting canopies, also the bridge linking the former station to the village of Halton on the opposite bank of the river. This bridge was built in 1869 by the Midland Railway to replace an earlier wooden one washed away by the river.

Continue on the trackbed past the station buildings and turn right on the narrow road to the bridge. Cross this structure, known locally as the "Penny Bridge" from earlier days when there was a toll, noting the view downstream to the M6 bridge whose traffic is usually all too audible. Once over the bridge, turn right at the Public Footpath sign

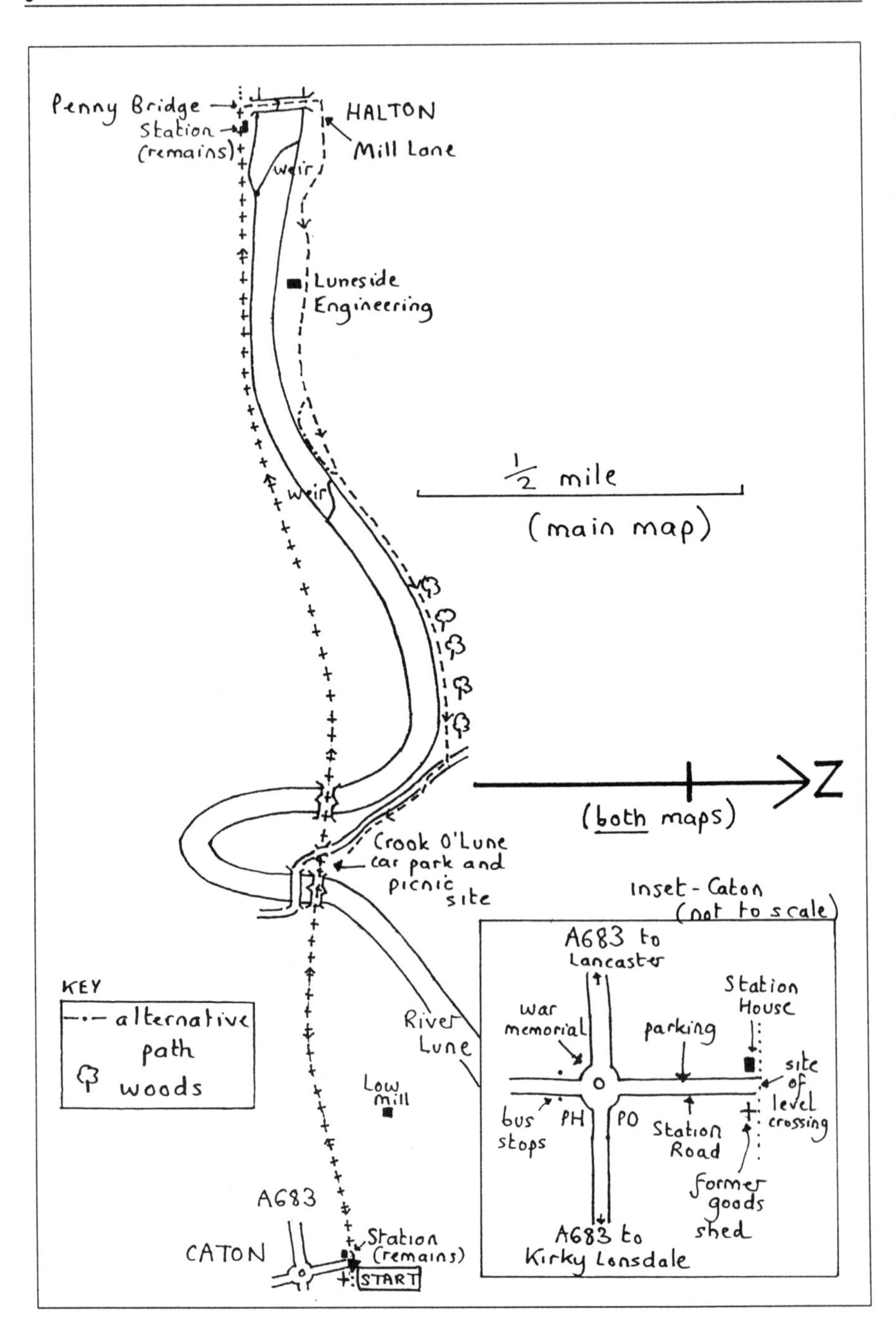
Penny Bridge
Station (remains)
HALTON
Mill Lane
weir
Luneside Engineering
½ mile
(main map)
weir
Z
(both maps)
Crook O'Lune car park and picnic site
Inset - Caton (not to scale)
A683 to Lancaster
Station House
war memorial
parking
site of level crossing
bus stops
PH
PO
Station Road
former goods shed
A683 to Kirkby Lonsdale
KEY
alternative path
woods
River Lune
Low Mill
A683
CATON
Station (remains)
START

into Mill Lane. Keep on this track, passing remains on the right of the former Halton Cotton Mill and swinging right at a squat modern mill (now a garage). Continue straight on past housing, the creeper-covered Luneside Engineering Co. building and more workshops to forbidding and rusty gates. Steps at the right of these allow further progress with the river's turbulent stretch (over the old weirs) visible below. Above the far bank, the course of the railway can clearly be seen on a stone embankment. The track narrows to a path which soon gives a choice of routes. A right fork leads down to the riverside with another forbidding gate and a stone slab floor left from the demolished Forse Bank Mill. Just past this is one end of the modern weir, where wooden steps lead up left to rejoin the main path. However, the last few metres between the steps and the main path are quite badly eroded, though passable with care. The left fork along the main path might thus be preferred, as it keeps to the hillside, crosses a ladder stile and winds through tall gorse bushes to a point above the steps.

Now the route follows a pleasant riverside path through the meadows with the noise from the weir receding behind. Cross a small footbridge, then a larger one leading into woods. The well-maintained path at first continues next to the river, but then climbs quite steeply up above the river bend to reach a road. Turn right on the road, with a view left to the former Low Mill at Caton (originally an 18th-century water-powered cotton-spinning mill) and over to a wind farm on the outer slopes of Bowland. The path soon becomes separate at the left of the road and leads down to the car park at Crook O'Lune – a busy spot at summer weekends . It is worth pausing at its picnic site, as here the view of the Lune valley is at its best, with Ingleborough prominent in the distance (if clear!). Descend steps from the picnic site/car park to regain the railway line which can be followed over the five-span viaduct and back into Caton.

2. By the Lune Estuary

Glasson Dock

A level stroll by the Lune a couple of miles before it enters Morecambe Bay combines branches of both the canal and the railway that were built to reach the small port at Glasson Dock.

Start: The car park at Conder Green picnic area. GR 457561.

Distance: 5km (just over 3 miles) on completely level terrain.

Map: Pathfinder 659 "Galgate and Dolphinholme".

By car: The picnic site is sign-posted off the A588 Lancaster-Blackpool road at the Stork pub, about three miles south of Lancaster. From outside the area, the best access is from junction 33 on the M6, taking the A6 south for about a mile and a quarter. A lane to the right is sign-posted "Glasson Dock". This lane leads to the B5272. Turn right on this into the village of Cockerham to meet the A588 which can be followed north for two and a half miles to the lane for Conder Green picnic site (see inset map 1).

By public transport: There is a limited bus service from Lancaster passing the Stork pub at Conder Green.

The background to this walk has to begin with Glasson Dock itself. This was first developed by the Lancaster Port Commissioners in the eighteenth century as an outport for Lancaster due to problems with the Lune at that location. By 1800, a sea wall, quays and a dock for 25 ships had all been built. Trade prospered until the middle of the nineteenth century, when the railways and port developments at Preston and Heysham put Glasson into a decline which continued until the 1980s. Since then there has been some revival of coastal trade (chiefly fertiliser and animal feeds), plus ship repair, but most maritime activity at Glasson now concerns yachting.

The canal was built in 1826 as a three-mile branch from the Lancaster Canal near Galgate. Six locks were constructed along the route, with a seventh between the previously built dock and a large basin at the end of the canal. There was a great deal of transshipment between coastal vessels and canal barges, and even some through traffic on the canal to Kendal and Preston, but now the canal is used only by pleasure craft.

The railway arrived in 1883 as a five-mile branch from Lancaster Castle station. It was built by the LNWR and there were stations at Glasson and Conder Green (where the picnic site is now), plus a private platform for Ashton Hall to the north. Passenger services ended in 1930 but there was a daily goods train up to 1947, and final closure did not come until 1964. In the 1970s much of the route was used by Lancashire County Council for a Lune Estuary Path, part of which forms the first section of this walk. It is possible to follow the railway in the other direction, towards Lancaster, for over two miles.

A busy scene at Glasson Dock *(Gordon Suggitt)*

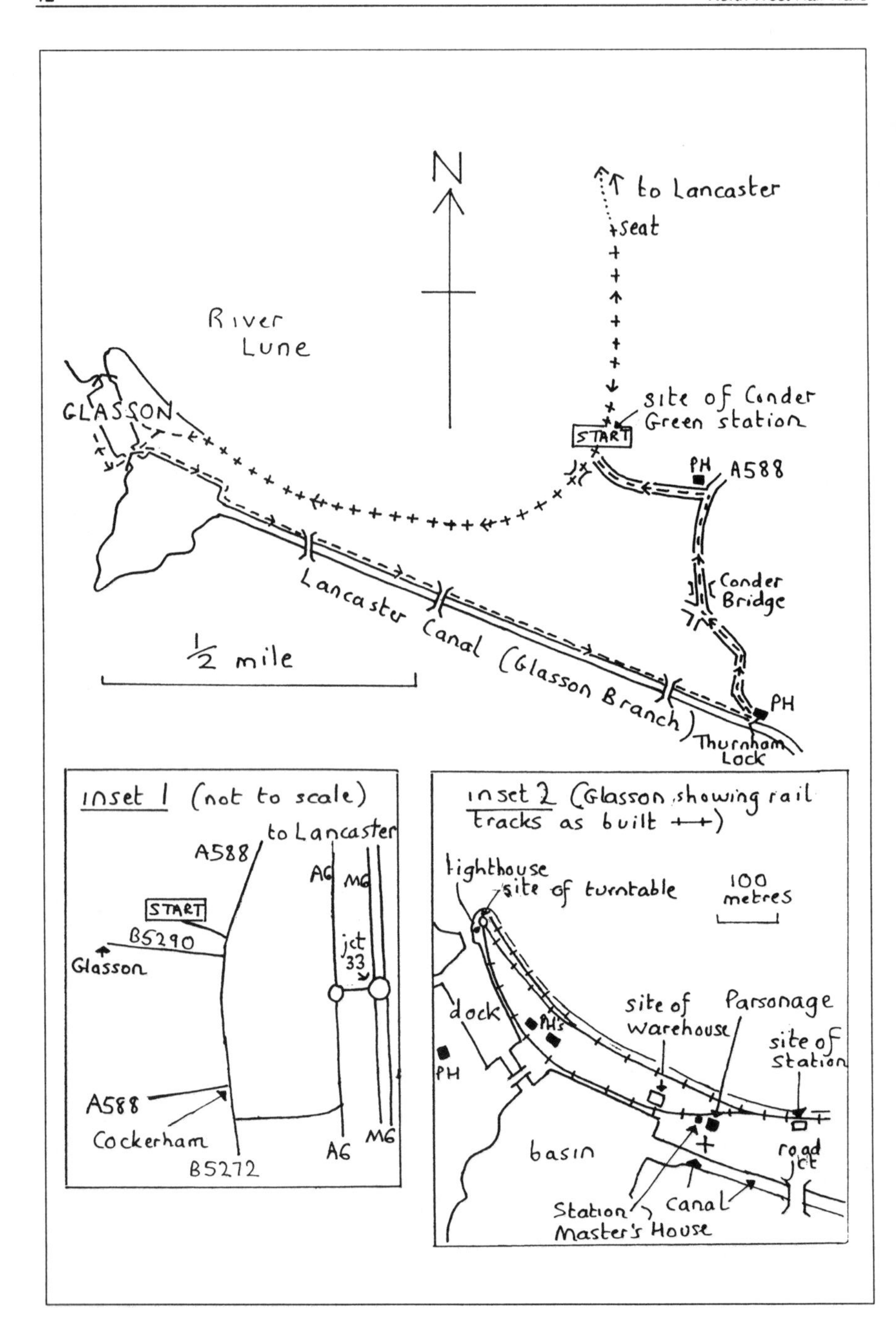
N
to Lancaster
seat
site of Conder Green station
START
PH
A588
River Lune
GLASSON
Conder Bridge
1/2 mile
Lancaster Canal (Glasson Branch)
PH
Thurnham Lock
inset 1 (not to scale)
to Lancaster
A588
A6
M6
START
B5290
Glasson
jct 33
A588
Cockerham
B5272
A6
M6
inset 2 (Glasson showing rail tracks as built)
lighthouse
site of turntable
100 metres
dock
PH's
PH
site of warehouse
Parsonage
site of station
basin
road jct
Station Master's House
canal

The Walk

Head back to the entrance of the car park, passing the Crossing Keeper's Cottage which is all that is left of Conder Green station except for the two crossing gate posts still in their stone turning mounts. These are by the "Lancashire Coastal Way" sign-post which indicates the start of the trackbed proper. Follow this across the railway bridge over the River Conder, with views (if clear) left to the hills of Bowland and right to the Lake District mountains. The route then crosses a second much smaller bridge as it curves gently right towards Glasson.

Just past a gate and a further bridge over a tiny channel, and almost across from the T-junction on the nearby road access to Glasson (left turn for West Quay, Yacht Marina, etc) is the site of Glasson station. This was well away from the settlement and nothing remains except for the Station Master's House. This too was away from the station, and is a modest building on the far side of the road, next to the more imposing Parsonage. A branch of the rail line crossed the road here and ran alongside the canal basin and dock. This cannot be traced, but the line used thus far can be followed for another 300 metres towards the boatyards, before it too ends between the bowling green and the Victoria Inn. This originally continued as two tracks to the right of the inn, one reaching the navigable part of the Lune, the other meeting the track from alongside the basin and dock at a turntable just beyond the lighthouse (see inset map 2). It is worth continuing a little further into Glasson itself which has cafes and pubs, and quite often, commercial activity in and around the dock. This does limit access on both sides of the dock, but the bridge over the lock can be crossed, towards the Dalton Arms, so that views can be had of the dock entrance and the tiny white lighthouse to its right.

Retrace the route back over the lock and head alongside the basin, now chiefly used for yachts. At the far end of the car park on the left stood a five-storey warehouse of which no trace remains. At the far end of the basin, take the path sign-posted "Canal Main Line, Lancaster, Garstang" to follow the canal towpath past Glasson's church on the left to the first bridge. Through this, in clear weather, the main range of hills of the Forest of Bowland can be seen looming ahead over the canal. The route now follows the canal towpath on a relentlessly straight stretch under two more bridges. Eventually Thurnham Lock appears ahead with its former mill on the left, now a pub and restaurant. (This was built as a water-powered corn mill predating the canal and in the 1960s was still worked using a 1924 turbine which had replaced the water-wheel.) Past the former mill, the canal curves away right in a shallow cutting, but the route leaves the towpath and follows the pub access road past the farm and left to the A588 at Conder Bridge. Turn right over the bridge and along to the Stork, where a left into the lane leads back to the starting point (note the fine Conder Green Farm on the right of the lane).

It is worth continuing past the end of the lengthy car park for another 400 metres or so along the trackbed to a strategically placed seat. Along this stretch there are fine views over the Lune estuary and, if clear, to the Lake District mountains. Past the seat, the track heads inland for a stretch so this is a suitable place to turn back to the car park once more.

3. In the Borderlands

Earby

Up to 1974, the whole of this walk would have been in Yorkshire. Even now the views on the return journey along part of the Pendle Way will (if clear) be towards the hills of the Yorkshire Dales.

Start: The small N.E. Lancs (formerly Yorkshire) town of Earby. GR square 9046.

Distance: 6.35km (almost 4 miles) with 60 metres (nearly 200 ft) of ascent on the return journey. See NOTE.

Map: Outdoor Leisure 21 "South Pennines" alternatively Pathfinder 670 "Barnoldswick and Earby".

By car: It is best to use Earby's central (though rather well-hidden) car park. Turn off the A56 Colne-Skipton road into Victoria Road at the signs for the bus station. Within 100 metres a sign points right to the free car park behind the houses and shops of Victoria Road.

By public transport: There are regular bus services to Earby bus station from Manchester, Burnley and Skipton. Leave the bus station by turning right, then once over the stream, right again into Valley Road.

NOTE: The former Colne-Skipton line is very much "the one that got away" from the walker's point of view. The Landranger map shows nearly 8km (5 miles) from Colne to Earby as a footpath. Unfortunately much of this is difficult to walk. It was earmarked by the county council for a Colne-Foulridge-Earby bypass for the A56, which has not, so far, been built. Thus although public access is allowed, the route has not been maintained and particularly close to Colne is waterlogged and overgrown. This walk uses the northernmost part of this section where this is less of a problem. In addition, the section north from the former Earby station past the present county boundary near Thornton-in-Craven is privately owned. 700 metres of this section are included on this walk (Lincoln Road to the station site). The use of this does not appear to be a problem, but if

Earby's "Museum of Yorkshire Dales Lead Mining" *(Gordon Suggitt)*

there are difficulties, the nearby A56 can be walked instead. Thus, the rail route of this walk is not as well-maintained as some others in this book. Also the return journey uses part of the Pendle Way across fields which can be wet and muddy. Altogether this is perhaps a walk for the more adventurous!

Although the East Lancashire Railway opened what now is Colne's only surviving rail link in 1849, it found itself second in the town to the Leeds and Bradford Railway, which had built its line from Skipton the previous year. This was soon absorbed by the Midland Railway for whom Colne was thus one of only three incursions into north-west England (the others were the line to Lancaster, Morecambe and Heysham – see Walk 1 – and the lines through Derbyshire into Manchester Central). Despite some early Manchester-Ilkley trains, regular through passenger services at Colne mostly ended with the opening in 1880 of the Blackburn-Hellifield link to the Midland's Settle and Carlisle line. Colne thus reverted to an end-on junction for two separate rail systems, although goods trains and summer excursions continued through workings. Midland services from Skipton called at intermediate stations at Elslack, Thornton, Earby and Foulridge, and there was a short branch to Barnoldswick (1871 -1965/6). Closures began with Elslack station in 1952, and the whole Skipton to Colne line shut in 1970, leaving Colne as the end of the line from Blackburn and Preston.

The Walk

Head out of the far end of the car park and turn left alongside the stream. Cross Victoria Road into Valley Road and keep going with the stream to the right, and the ends of Albion Street and Lincoln Road on the left, to reach a crossroads by the "Yorkshire Dales Museum of Lead Mining". This is housed in a fine old building with some exhibits (water wheel, rail wagon etc) visible even when the museum is closed (its current opening hours are Wednesday and Friday-Sunday 1-5pm, Thursday 1-8pm, from the end of March to the end of October). Turn left up School Lane to reach the main road (A56) at the former level crossing. To the right the railway continued towards Skipton, but turn left and after the garden the line becomes accessible opposite the end of Lincoln Road (see **NOTE** above).

The line now heads south above the main road and works on the left and a recreation ground to the right. Cross a bridge over a lane, after which trees screen modern factory units on the left. Towards the end of these is an older building which is the unmistakable goods shed of the former Earby station. This occupied the next 200 metres of the route, but nothing remains except hummocky remnants of platforms in a rather wet stretch ending at a road, with the Station Hotel of 1898 away to the left on the main road.

Cross the road and continue south along the trackbed which is soon above the main road allowing a view left to the moors above Kelbrook before it is hidden by trees. Next is a lengthy stretch above the backs of the houses of Sough, with signs of former quarrying on the right. Garden extensions encroach from the left until the trackbed opens out once more. Now the route is in a shallow cutting with a ruined wayside shelter on the right. A bridge over a lane and stream allows views this time to the moors away to the right, above Barnoldswick, before the former branch to that town can be seen

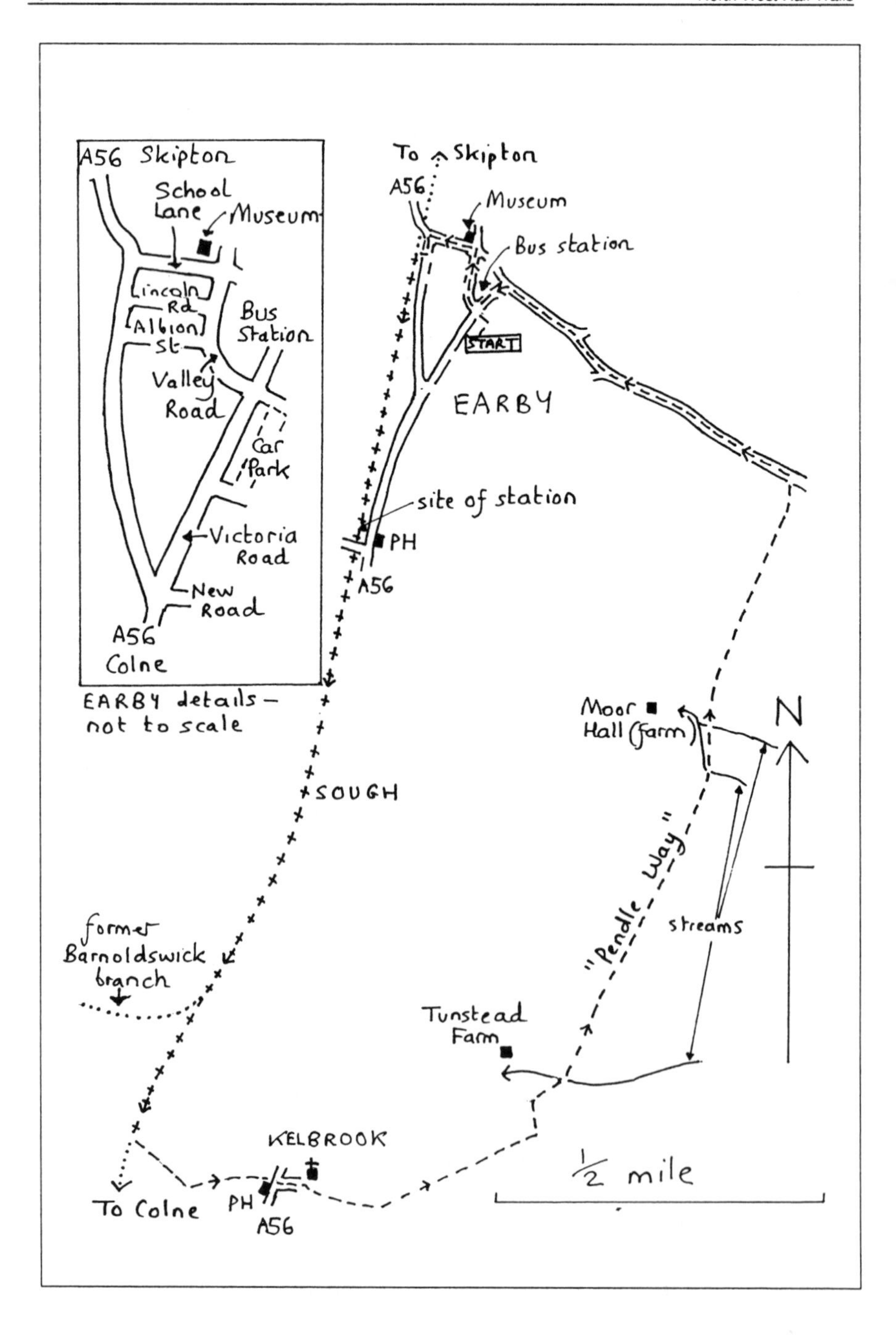
A56 Skipton
School Lane
Museum
Lincoln Rd
Albion St
Bus Station
Valley Road
Car Park
Victoria Road
New Road
A56 Colne
EARBY details – not to scale
To Skipton
A56
Museum
Bus station
START
EARBY
site of station
PH
A56
SOUGH
former Barnoldswick branch
Moor Hall (farm)
N
"Pendle Way"
streams
Tunstead Farm
KELBROOK
To Colne
PH
A56
½ mile

heading away to the right on an embankment. This is soon fenced-off and unwalkable, so keep on the route south towards Colne on a potentially wet stretch (the worst of this can be avoided by a drier path through the trees on the right). Cross a farm track and within 200 metres watch out for steps off the railway on the left up to a "Right of Way" marker post. (This is 120 metres **before** the road bridge which carries the Barnoldswick road (B6383) over the railway).

Go up these steps on the left, over a stile and along the left edge of a field on a clear path to another stile. Cross this onto a gravel path which swings left past a football pitch on the right to the access lane for the fine Victorian vicarage on the left. Follow the lane down to the A56 where the Craven Heifer pub is on the right. Cross the main road into Vicarage Road and over the stream to the church. Turn right and do not recross the stream but carry on with it on the right through the oldest part of Kelbrook. Here is the first of the Pendle Way signs (with a black outline of a witch) which are invaluable for route-finding on the rest of the walk where they are referred to as PW signs.

Pass attractive cottages, then swing away from the stream past a 1990 date stone on a house's garage to the right. Carry straight on up the bridleway between Craven Game Farm (left) and a pebbledashed farm with its builder's name carved above the door (right). Continue over a cattle grid and up the surfaced lane, passing a seat in the field on the left. After the slope has levelled off, a broad grassy track comes in from the left (with PW signs). Go left on this track and just before a new gate bear right on a boardwalk raised above wet and muddy stretches. At the end of this cross a stile into a drier field and continue with a fence on the left. By now there should be views of Kelbrook Moor to the right. In 50 metres, just past rowan and holly trees on the left, turn left to a gate with its PW sign hidden by another rowan tree. (Do **not** continue uphill to the right of the stream). Go through the gate towards prominent trees, passing through a small gate (PW signs) to two large isolated trees. Views ahead and left now include Earby and the valley followed by the railway, although the actual line is obscured by houses. If clear, the more distant views include the Forest of Bowland to the far left, then round to Ingleborough and straight ahead Great Whernside.

Keep going on a track slightly sunk into the hillside as it bears right to a gate with a stone stile (PW sign). Cross this and continue with a fence now on the left. Keep above the farm (Moor Hall) further down to the left by passing through a gate and along a track with a small gully (left). After a tiny stream, the track heads left downhill towards distant bungalows. Do **not** follow this but instead strike across the hillside to cross a partly infilled gully with gorse and rowan trees to a wooden stile (PW sign). Cross this and continue now with a fence on the right towards stone cottages. The path now becomes a clearer track to these cottages where a left turn at PW signs leads onto a tarmac road. This is usually quite traffic-free and leads past pleasantly varied housing down into Earby. Keep on the "main" road as indicated by the road markings past the "Holiday Cottages Group" offices and Earby Library, and fork left at the Conservative Club into Victoria Road for the bus station and car park.

4. Across the Ribble

Preston Junction

Two crossings of the Ribble are included in this walk, which is almost entirely on tarmac paths in parkland and countryside immediately south of Preston.

Start: On Carrwood Way, Walton Park (about two miles south of Preston town centre). GR 547269.

Distance: 4.6km (just under 3 miles) with 33 metres (100 ft) of climb.

Map: Pathfinder 688 " Preston (South) and Leyland".

By car: At the A6 roundabout with the B6230 (about 1½ miles south of Preston town centre) take the exit sign-posted "Walton Park". In half a mile, turn left at a smaller roundabout into Carrwood Way. Park about 250 yards along Carrwood Way, at the left of the road by the "No Through Road" signs.

By public transport: The nearest access by bus to the start would be the Preston to Leyland service (via Bamber Bridge), which has stops close to the smaller roundabout, near to the start of Carrwood Way. Alternatively, the route could easily be reached at Avenham Park, which is only about 600 metres from Preston Railway Station. Access from Preston Bus Station would be more difficult, involving a walk of about 1.2km across the town centre.

It may seem surprising to encounter the East Lancashire Railway this far west in the county. Here in 1847 it was allowed its own route into Preston for its line from Blackburn, which had originally used the North Union Railway lines for the last 2½ miles. This left the previous route at Bamber Bridge and ran NW to cross the Ribble into Preston by its own bridge, reached by a 52-arch viaduct across the floodplain. This proved so unstable that in 1886 it was replaced by the present embankment. There was one station on the branch, the confusingly named Preston Junction station (Todd Lane from 1952). This junction allowed ELR trains to also use the branch for Preston-Liverpool services. The branch layout was further complicated by the Lancashire and Yorkshire Railway (which had absorbed the ELR in 1859) building two more junctions at Whitehouse. The South junction was built in 1883 for Blackburn-Southport services, and the North one opened for Preston to Southport trains in 1900. Having opened last, these were the first to close in 1964-5, followed by the whole branch for passengers in 1968 and for goods four years later. Now Blackburn-Preston trains once more use the former North Union rails into Preston. Work to develop the former railway as a nature reserve was begun in 1990 by Lancashire County Council, who publish a useful leaflet "Preston Junction Local Nature Reserve".

Three hundred yards upstream from the former railway bridge across the Ribble is a second bridge. It is known locally as the "Old Tram Bridge", although it is a replacement for the original tramway bridge. This was built in 1803 as part of a five-mile link between the northern and southern sections of the Lancaster Canal. These had been built in 1792-9 from Lancaster to Preston and Clayton to Chorley (later extended to Wigan by agreement with the Leeds and

The Old Tram Bridge, looking towards the Italianate villas of 1847 above Avenham Park *(Gordon Suggitt)*

Liverpool Canal). The tramway was intended as a temporary stop-gap until the canal was built across the Ribble, but this was never done. It was worked by horses pulling up to six wagons at a time, except at the steep north bank of the Ribble, where a stationary engine was used. The tramway closed in 1857, but its route is still walkable for nearly two miles from Avenham Park in Preston to Todd Lane North.

The Walk

Turn right from Carrwood Way at the blue "Leyland" cycleway sign, and go down the lane with Leigh House Farm to the left and new housing on the right. At the bottom of the slope is the railway which crosses the lane on a red brick bridge. Go right just before the bridge to reach the track through wooden gates. To the left, the former rail route heads away to the site of Preston Junction (Todd Lane) station, where no remains are visible, and the junction for lines to Blackburn and Liverpool. This is a comparatively featureless stretch, so instead the route chosen goes in the opposite direction (right). The track bends gently right between willow trees for 800 metres until the shallow cutting suddenly ends overlooking the Old Tram Road. There are massive mills to the left and views of Preston straight ahead, as the path drops down through two sets of gates, and climbs back up to the embankment which continues along to the Ribble. Now activity can usually be seen on the West Coast Main Line on its embankment further to the left.

Soon the start of the triangular Whitehouse Junction (built for Southport trains) is reached, just as the path drops down once more for a missing bridge. Passing through gateways either side of a lane, the path climbs back again onto the embankment with a stretch of rough gravel leading towards the Ribble. The Old Tram Bridge is visible over to the right below the buildings of central Preston. Ignore the tarmac path down to the river and instead head for the fenced-off railway bridge. Despite the uninviting spikes, there is access to a walkway at the right of the grassed-over railway track. There are views of the main line bridge just further downstream as the broad tidal Ribble is crossed.

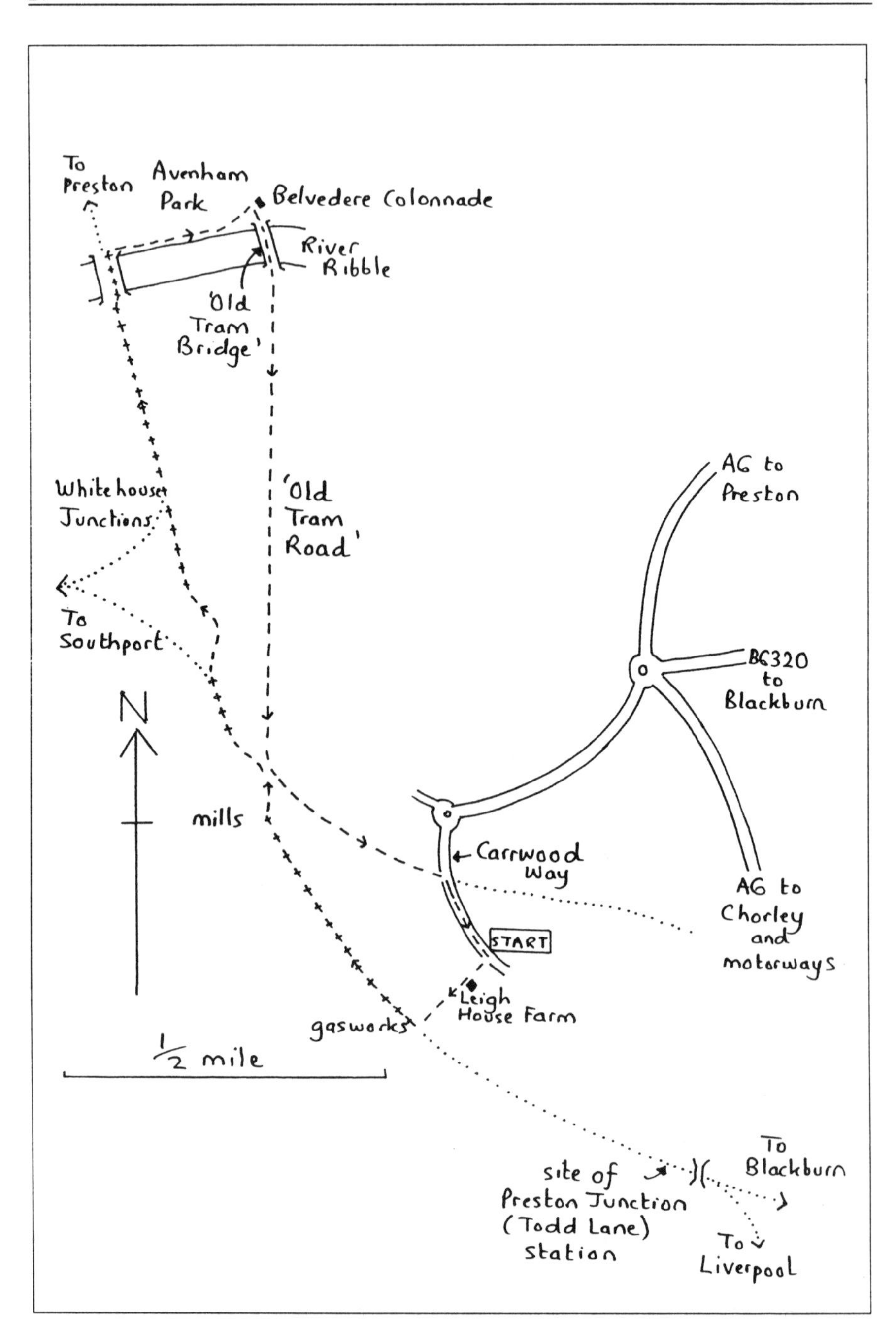
To Preston
Avenham Park
Belvedere Colonnade
River Ribble
'Old Tram Bridge'
'Old Tram Road'
Whitehouse Junctions
To Southport
N
mills
gasworks
1/2 mile
A6 to Preston
B6320 to Blackburn
Carrwood Way
START
Leigh House Farm
A6 to Chorley and motorways
site of Preston Junction (Todd Lane) station
To Blackburn
To Liverpool

Immediately after the bridge descend the steps, and turn right to reach the riverside. Downstream is the bridge just crossed, with brick arches either side of the river which are all that is left of the original 1850 viaduct. Further left is the embankment which replaced most of the other arches, while the bridge itself dates from 1930. Continue upstream through Avenham Park, built in the 1860s to provide work for unemployed cotton workers during the American Civil War. Head towards the Old Tram Bridge, but before it go left up the steps to the imposing "Belvedere Colonnade". The level area in front of this is the site of the engine house, which hauled wagons up from the tram bridge by cable.

From the colonnade, head steeply down to the Old Tram Bridge. Here the embankment for the former rail route can be seen on the right stretching away to the mills. Cross the bridge and enter the long avenue of trees marking the tramway route as it heads towards the railway. As the two almost join, it is possible to finish by retracing the first part of the outward journey. The full route however keeps on the Old Tram Road bearing left, up above bungalows, to become an "official" walking and cycling route which crosses Carrwood Way 250 metres from the start of the walk.

5. With the "Union"

Abbey Village

The former railway section of this walk is largely enclosed in cuttings, but the return journey is on higher ground with potential views across to the West Pennine Moors, Pendle Hill, etc.

Start: The eastern end of Withnell Nature Reserve at Abbey Village. GR 640228.

Distance: 4.6km (just under 3 miles) with 57 metres (185 feet) of climb, mostly on quite a steep pull out of Brinscall.

Map: Explorer 19 "West Pennine Moors", alternatively Pathfinder 689 "Blackburn".

By car: Abbey Village is on the A675 between Preston and Bolton, just over a mile south of junction 3 on the M65. The entrance to the nature reserve is at the extreme north of the village. Coming from the M65, watch out for the 30mph signs. Eighty metres beyond these, take the first right down the former station approach road. Pass the station building on the right, and as the nature reserve gate approaches there is parking for 3-4 cars on the right. Coming from the Bolton direction, the entrance is at the far end of the village, just past the Royal pub. (There is a small sign visible from this direction but it is easily missed.)

By public transport: There is a regular bus service between Chorley and Blackburn which passes through Abbey Village (alight at the Royal pub), but it is more frequent at Brinscall (the halfway point on the walk) which thus might be better used for a start and finish.

The Lancashire Union Railway was formed in 1863 to build lines from Blackburn to Wigan and St Helens. The section from Blackburn to Chorley was built jointly by the LUR and the Lancashire and Yorkshire Railway and opened in 1869. It left the Blackburn to Preston line west of Cherry Tree and passed through intermediate stations at Feniscowles, Withnell, Brinscall and Heapey. The line was eight and a half miles long and rose to a summit of nearly 600 feet at Brinscall (the midpoint of this walk). Closure for passengers came in 1960 and for goods six years later. Almost the only notable feature left is the Three Arch Bridge over the A674 on the western approaches to Blackburn, although station buildings survive at Withnell and Heapey.

The former Withnell station building, now a private residence. *(Gordon Suggitt)*

The Walk

Go through the gate into the nature reserve whose presence is soon indicated by signs such as "species-rich neutral grassland". The path is now on the former trackbed in a shallow cutting. After crossing a tiny stream twice, an imposing overbridge looms ahead as the cutting becomes deeper. The only gap in the enclosing sides is on the left as a fenced-off branch comes in from the former mill at Abbey Village, closed in the 1970s. Housing now begins to appear high on the right, indicating the start of Withnell, whose main street crosses the line by a massive smoke-blackened bridge (almost three times the width of the road it carries). 100 metres after the bridge, the nature reserve ends at another gate, but the route continues ahead to

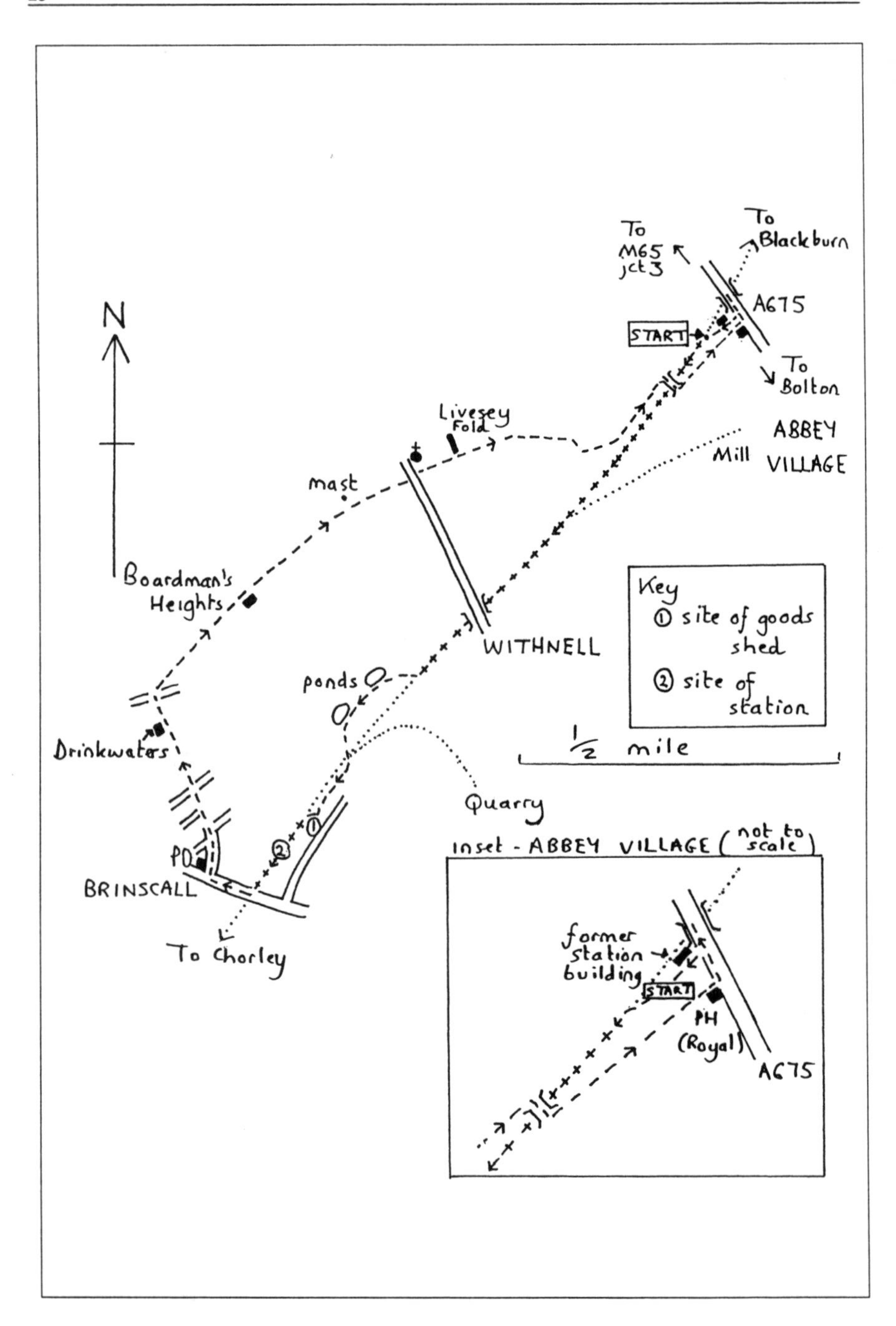
N
To M65 jct 3
To Blackburn
A675
START
To Bolton
ABBEY VILLAGE
Mill
Livesey Fold
mast
Boardman's Heights
WITHNELL
Key
① site of goods shed
② site of station
½ mile
ponds
Drinkwaters
Quarry
PO
BRINSCALL
To Chorley
inset - ABBEY VILLAGE (not to scale)
former station building
START
PH (Royal)
A675

join a path entering from the right. At first, this too follows the trackbed, but in another 125 metres it heads away right to two ponds used for angling, occupying a former quarry. After the second pond, the path swings right round a grassy knoll then left across the route of the railway, now grassed over. Around this point, a branch went off left into the main Withnell Quarry.

After another 200 metres of landscaped areas, the path turns left at a dogs "scoop" bin to a road on the left. The site of the goods shed of the former Brinscall station was over to the right, by the road. The setting of the villages of Withnell and Brinscall is also clear at this point, with the start of high moorland away to the left. Do not follow the path from here, instead head diagonally right from the bin, across what can be a rather soggy grassed-over area to meet a fence coming from the right at a line of young trees along a ditch. Here the route is back on the line of the railway, as can be seen by the embankment end straight ahead. Follow the fence straight ahead, passing the site of Brinscall station building and platforms, now completely landscaped over. The exit from this stretch is by gateposts onto Brinscall's main street, with the embankment above marking the railway's course towards Chorley (this is not walkable).

Turn right to walk up the hill past some of Brinscall's older houses. After 75 metres, turn right just before the Post Office into Withnell Fold Old Road. Follow this road up as it curves left to newer housing. As the tarmac turns right into Heather Lea Drive, carry straight on up the slope on a rough track. After 75 metres, at the end of Chapel Street, this becomes a path but continue on it up the hill, crossing another road and passing on the left the remains of the old Drinkwaters farm, now engulfed by modern housing. 60 metres after the farm, the path ends at a road. Cross this to a rough track heading diagonally right (with a public footpath sign). Follow the track along to the renovated farm buildings of Boardman's Heights. By now, the views have opened up towards the still-working Withnell Quarry and the moors above it. If clear, Darwen Tower will be seen to the left of the view and the tallest TV mast on Winter Hill on the right.

Ignore the track off to the left at Boardman's Heights, and pass next to the buildings to reach a gate with a public footpath sign and a clear track ahead. This leads towards a telephone mast and a strangely pagoda-like church spire. By the mast is a good point to look back and see the route followed by the former railway en route for Chorley. Continue through a gate to reach the top of Withnell's main street. Cross this diagonally left to a public footpath sign pointing to a track alongside the churchyard and then the end of a terrace (Livesey Fold). Now the view ahead is towards Abbey Village, dominated by its former mill, and to the left (if clear) the M65 motorway and Pendle Hill with, further left, Longridge Fell and Bowland.

Continue downhill towards the railway, whose course NE to Blackburn can just be made out. At a small gateway, the path clearly heads diagonally right across the field to gateposts with a track beyond. Follow this as it joins another track from the right to go alongside the railway, with a convenient seat for the view. Cross over the bridge passed under on the outward journey, and immediately after it turn left on a path above the railway (sign-posted "No Cycling. No Horse Riding.") Keep on the path as it swings right into a straight stretch along to the A675 at the Royal. Turn left on this road, and walk past the station approach to the bridge over the railway. The view left over the station is well worthwhile, when not obscured by foliage, but on the other side the line towards Blackburn, although visible, is not walkable. Return to the station approach and walk past the building of Withnell Station (so named despite being at Abbey Village) to the starting point.

6. Along the loop

Rishton

Although only three miles NE of central Blackburn, this walk is mostly in pleasant rural surroundings, and combines a lesser rail link with part of the much more famous Leeds and Liverpool Canal.

Start: By the Leeds and Liverpool Canal (bridge 108) at the end of Spring Street, Rishton. GR 728308.

Distance: 4.6km (just under 3 miles) on mostly level terrain.

Map: Explorer 19 "West Pennine Moors" alternatively Pathfinder 680 "Great Harwood and Longridge".

By car: Spring Street leads north from the A678 in Rishton (see inset map). Coming from the Blackburn direction, it is the third street on the left after the traffic lights for the B6535 to Great Harwood, just past the post office and the Roebuck pub. Coming the other way, it is the first street on the right after the humpback bridge over the canal.

Proceed along Spring Street past typical Lancashire terraced housing for 400 metres until new housing appears ahead. Do not drive into the new estate but instead bear right on an unsurfaced track which soon crosses a narrow bridge over the canal. Immediately past this on the left there is a small car park.

By public transport: The start of the walk is not easily reached by bus. However, the "Hyndburn Circular" service from Blackburn and Accrington bus stations allows a start to be made from the B6535 close to the canal. This service also allows access to the "Extra" walk.

The North Lancashire Loop railway ran for 9 miles from Great Harwood Junction east of Blackburn to Rose Grove west of Burnley. It formed an alternative route through the small towns of Great Harwood and Padiham rather than the more direct link via Accrington, and was built by the Lancashire and Yorkshire Railway. Completion took five years to achieve (1877) as construction was difficult and expensive due to unstable earthworks. Passenger services to the stations at Great Harwood, Simonstone and Padiham lasted only 80 years, with goods services on the section walked ending in 1964.

The most memorable feature on the line is the Martholme viaduct, with 10 stone spans 65 feet above the River Calder. This is about 3 miles NE of this walk (see map inset) and can be reached by a lane 500 metres north of the B6535/A680 junction, or by walking the line from Mill Lane (200 metres south of this junction). This second alternative has been included as an "Extra" to this walk.

The part of the Leeds and Liverpool Canal walked here belongs to a 24-mile stretch without locks between Blackburn and Barrowford. It was completed by 1816, and only one tunnel and one major embankment (both at Burnley) were required to keep this stretch level. However, to keep at a constant height of about 415 feet above sea level, a very winding course was needed. Although the length walked is comparatively straight, just to the east the canal almost doubles back on itself around Church.

A rail tour visits Padiham station in 1967, ten years after the last scheduled passenger services. *(J. Davenport)*

The Walk

From the car park, ignore the broad path heading out from its far end. Instead, bear right alongside a fence on the left. The path soon becomes a roughly surfaced track, heading towards Pendle Hill which is usually visible beyond the power lines. A small valley opens up on the left; the railway is just beyond its far slope. The path descends by a huge hedge to the historic hamlet of Tottleworth at a junction of tracks below a house with a multiple date stone for 1748 and 1970! Turn left on the rough lane, over two bridges, and up towards the railway which is reached at a bridge with a high narrow span. Go up the steps on the right of the bridge to reach the gravelled path on the former trackbed. This can be followed into Great Harwood by turning right, but the route has been landscaped beyond recognition. Instead, turn left and keep on the gravelled path bearing right where the trackbed goes straight on. The reason for this should soon be clear as the actual rail route becomes a muddy morass in a deepening cutting. The path keeps to the edge of the cutting as far as a junction of paths at a filled-in bridge over the railway.

Head right along the edge of the former rail route, which has been landscaped and covered with pylons. At least on the right is the identifiable slope of a cutting, then as the sign for the "Hyndburn Urban Forestry Project" is passed, a bridge can been seen ahead. Make for this, with a clearer trackbed appearing on the left, though as far as the bridge it is flooded and filled with rushes (the path keeps to drier land at the right). At the bridge, the trackbed is joined for its most recognizable stretch. At first, this is in a cutting, but this eases to give views over to hills scarred by quarrying on the right and the industrial outskirts of Blackburn ahead. The railway is now on a low embankment with the canal on the slope to the left. A bridge ahead for a farm track marks the end of the walkable stretch; in fact, the path leaves the trackbed to follow the top edge of the cutting leading to the bridge. Arriving at the track at the left of the bridge, the view over the far parapet shows how thoroughly the rail route west to Blackburn has been landscaped out of existence.

Turn left on the track towards the canal with, if clear, views towards distant hills. At the canal, cross the cattle grid and descend to a metal gate at the right of the bridge. Turn left on the towpath under

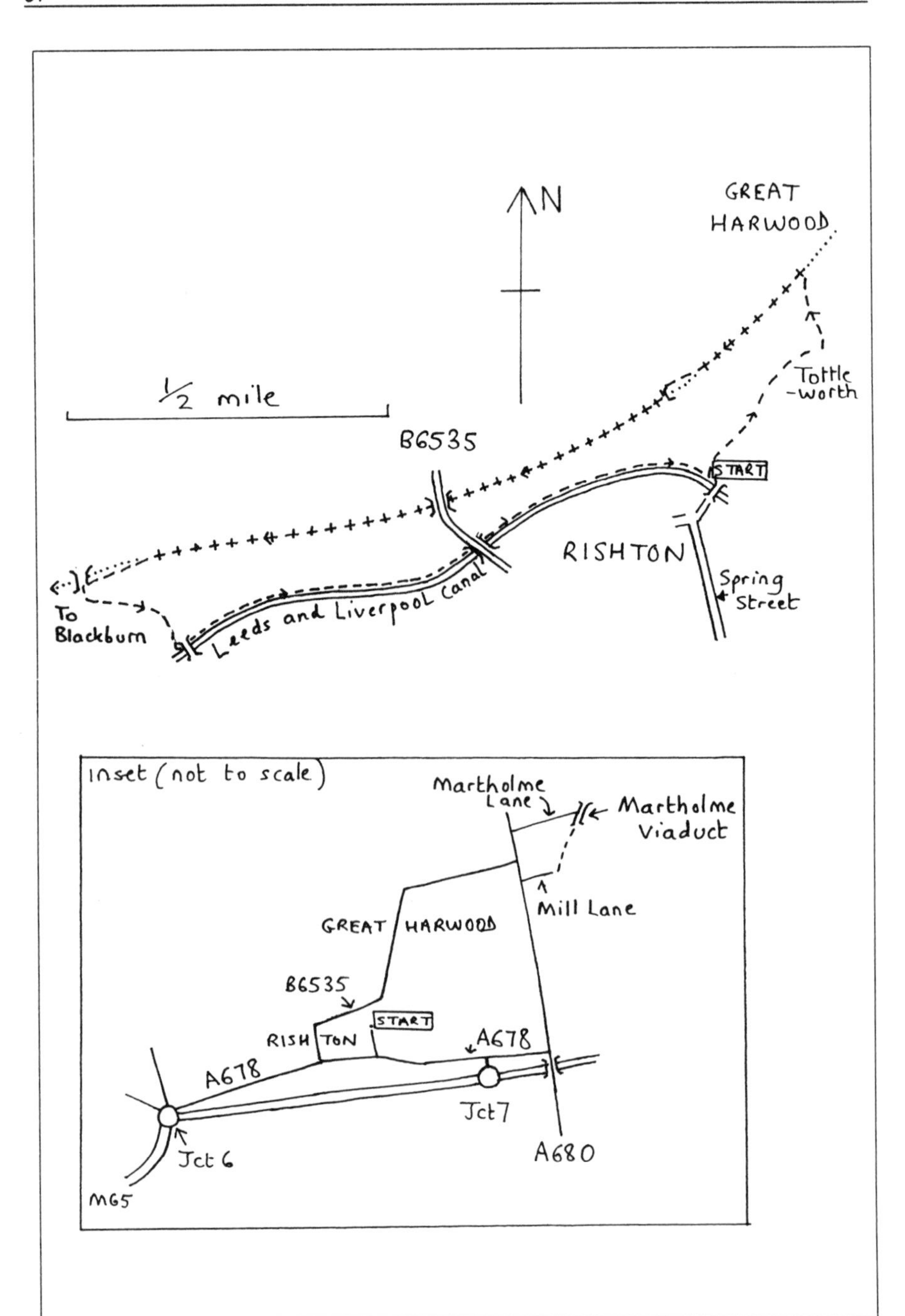
N
GREAT HARWOOD
½ mile
Tottle-worth
B6535
START
RISHTON
Spring Street
To Blackburn
Leeds and Liverpool Canal
Inset (not to scale)
Martholme Lane
Martholme Viaduct
Mill Lane
GREAT HARWOOD
B6535
START
RISHTON
A678
A678
Jct 7
Jct 6
A680
M65

the bridge and follow the canal as it winds gently towards Rishton, with Pendle Hill usually visible again over the railway embankment to the left. The canal heads under the power lines which have accompanied most of this route, then under the bridge for the B6535. After a cleared site on the left and allotments to the right, the canal swings right beneath new housing to the attractive arch of bridge 108 and the well-screened car park on the left.

Extra! Although too short at a little over one mile to count as a full walk, the stretch of line from Mill Lane to Martholme Viaduct is well worth including. Note that the route as described includes a flight of 73 steps. These can be avoided by walking straight along the embankment and back, but this means missing the views of the viaduct itself.

Go along Mill Lane for 300 metres from the A680 (see main walk and inset map). As the road dips, there is parking for several cars on the left, by the "Lancashire County Council" signs. Enter by the gateway on the left on the path which climbs straight onto the embankment, with views across the Calder Valley towards Burnley. After 120 metres, there is a drop then a climb back onto the level which continues all the way to the viaduct.

However, about 150 metres after the golf course on the left comes to an end, it is worth taking a clear path to the left, leading towards a white-gabled building. Pass this and ignore steps up to the golf course to gain the first views of the viaduct over to the right. The scanty remains of the former Martholme Colliery appear on the left, just before a gateway. Go through this and turn right along the road with impressive views of the viaduct looming ever closer. Eventually, just before the first span, a flight of 73 steps on the right leads up to the railway. Signs warn about "no access over bridge", but it should be possible to catch a glimpse of the 16th-century Martholme Gatehouse nestling by the River Calder. From here, it is a straightforward walk back along the embankment to the starting point.

7. Up the bank

Accrington to Baxenden

Within a half-mile of the centre of Accrington, there is public access to Baxenden Bank, formerly one of the most formidable obstacles on the rail network of NW England.

Start: Mount Street, Accrington (see inset map). GR 760279. **NOTE:** Although the current Explorer 19 map shows the start of the permitted path much closer to Accrington town centre at GR 758284, this section was not walkable by the end of 1998.

Distance: 4.6km (just under 3 miles) with 80 metres (260 feet) of climb. The "extension" adds an extra 1.5km (1 mile) with little extra height.

Map: Explorer 19 "West Pennine Moors", alternatively Pathfinder 689 "Blackburn".

By car: From Accrington town centre, take the A680 towards Manchester (sign-posted Baxenden and Haworth Art Gallery). Immediately before the Police Station, turn right into Spring Gardens. As the road bends right, turn left into Nuttall Street. Continue along this through the housing to the start of the factories on Mount Street. Park on the left-hand side of Nuttall Street as the housing ends.

By public transport: There are good bus and rail services to the centre of Accrington. From the stations, it is a little over a kilometre to the start (although the Accrington-Church Circular local service does travel along Nuttall Street). This will be reduced to less than 400 metres when access from the town centre is improved – see NOTE above. Alternatively, the route could be walked one-way to the site of Baxenden station with a return journey by bus along the A680 back to Accrington.

The Baxenden Bank was part of the East Lancashire Railway's extension from its Rossendale line at Stubbins to Accrington, built 1845-8. From the south, the line rose on a steady 1 in 78 gradient through Helmshore and Haslingden to its summit of 760 feet at Baxenden. From here, it was a drop of 280 feet in two and a quarter miles to Accrington Station, giving gradients as severe as 1 in 38 and

On Baxenden Bank near Priestley Clough.
(Gordon Suggitt)

1 in 40. This was the Baxenden Bank, regarded as one of the most difficult lines to work anywhere in the country. The ELR became part of the Lancashire and Yorkshire Railway in 1859, which in turn became part of the LNWR in 1921, shortly before the grouping of 1923. The Accrington Extension remained a busy line, both for passenger traffic especially on the Colne-Manchester commuter run, and for freight, notably cotton and coal. However, closures began with Baxenden station in 1951, followed by Haslingden in 1960. The whole line from Stubbins to Accrington closed in 1966, with its route past Haslingden now used for the A56 by-pass. For its features on the Helmshore-Stubbins stretch, see walks 8 and 9.

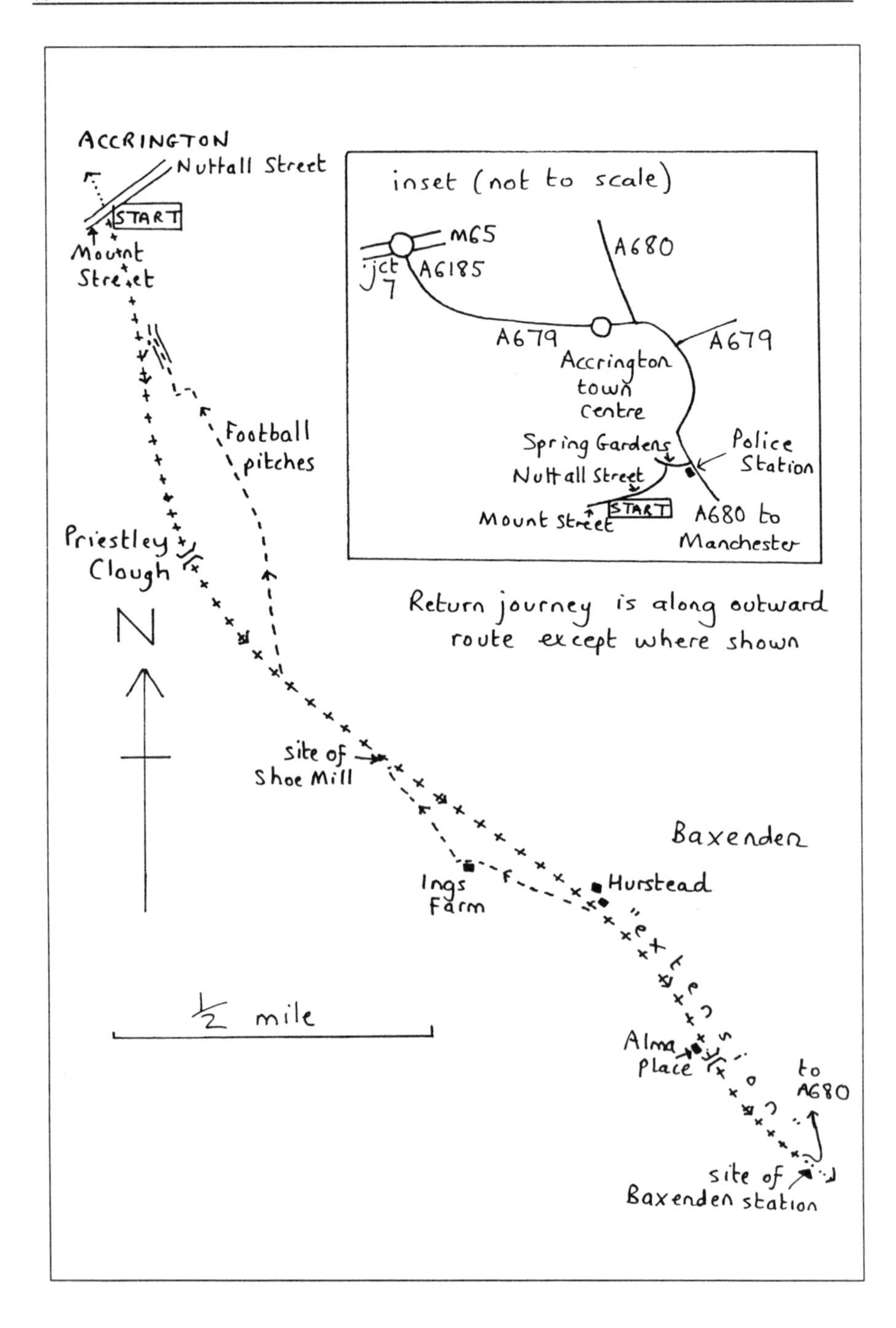
ACCRINGTON
Nuttall Street
START
Mount Street
Football pitches
Priestley Clough
N
site of Shoe Mill
Baxenden
Ings Farm
Hurstead
extension
Alma Place
to A680
site of Baxenden station
½ mile
inset (not to scale)
M65
jct 7
A6185
A680
A679
A679
Accrington town centre
Spring Gardens
Police Station
Nuttall Street
Mount Street
START
A680 to Manchester
Return journey is along outward route except where shown

The Walk

Entering at the "concessionary bridle way" post or through the decorative wooden arch (designed by the nearby Woodnook Primary School), there is an immediate sharp climb to compensate for the demolished bridge over Mount Street. The track curves right, past housing on the left and still-working mills on the right. The gradient eases somewhat as the route enters a deep cutting, eventually passing under the bridge for Priestley Clough. The climb continues steadily up until there is a dip for the now-demolished Shoe Mill viaduct, once seven arches of blue brick over the Woodnook water. The remains of Shoe Mill itself are down by the stream on the right and include the stump of the chimneystack. Despite its name, it was built in the late 18th century for the cotton industry. After the climb up from the replacement bridge, the cutting slowly diminishes until there are views left over the miniature gorge towards the church at Baxenden. A second dip for a missing bridge leads to the end of the official concessionary bridleway by the attractive cottages at Hurstead. By now, the route has climbed almost 200 feet of the Baxenden Bank.

Extension: Although not "official", the rail route is still quite walkable for another half-mile (800 metres), but is apt to be very wet and muddy in places. At first there is the site of Baxenden Quarry sidings parallel to the line on the right, then increasing settlement close to the line, including mill remains on the left and the strikingly black-and-white painted Alma Place to the right. Just below this is a wayside hut by the track side, then an inaccessible overbridge. Through a further gate, the line passes millponds and housing with a massive barn, before ending abruptly at the factory area for Holland's Pies. At this point, the start of Baxenden station's up-platform is in the undergrowth at the left.

Return: This rail remnant does not tie in well with other usable paths to make a circuit. There is no feasible alternative at all for the "extension", so this must be re-walked back to Hurstead. From there, two small diversions are possible, both giving fine views of the setting of the rail route.

Hurstead to Shoe Mill: Take the paved track left at Hurstead, ignoring the public footpath sign and stile, up to Ings Cottage, followed by Ings Farm and a jumble of sheds. Walk through these to a gate (sometimes open) giving access between a fence on the right and a small wooded valley to the left. A further gate leads into a open field with fine views back across the valley once used by the railway. Continue down the field to another gate in its bottom corner. Once through this, ignore an apparently clearer track leading left. Keeping instead to the wall on the right, go round its end (with a bit of detached fencing) and down to the railway just above the dip at Shoe Mill.

Shoe Mill to Mount Street: From the bridge, continue 400 metres along the track until, in a break between the cuttings, a wooden plank bridge leads across the ditch at the right. Go through the kissing-gate and head diagonally left up and across the field, towards the fence corner on the skyline. Passing just below this, three stiles appear in the fence ahead. Cross the middle one, and the track beyond it, to carry on straight ahead with scrubland to the left and the edge of a football pitch to the right. If it is clear, the full extent of the Forest of Bowland hills occupies the skyline. Proceed to the end of a second football pitch, where Accrington's terraced streets and remaining mills spread across the view. The railway route is over in the wooded valley to the left, though not as far below as seems likely. Turn left at the belt of trees ahead, and within 50 metres right onto a track by allotments leading into a housing estate. Take the left fork of roads and, after the first three buildings on the left, an open space reveals the rail route again. Descend the path at the end of the open space, by the fence corner, to reach the railway just before the descent past the mills to the starting point. The continuation of the railway down to Accrington station can be seen by the embankment between the factory car park and houses across the road, but this was not walkable by the end of 1998.

8. From the museum

Helmshore

This walk includes not just a disused railway but a real Rossendale mix – mills used as a museum, a quarry tramway, a reservoir dam, a detached chimney, workers' cottages, an abandoned farm and even the area's best-known firm!

Start: The Textile Museum at Higher Mill, Helmshore. GR 778215. The museum is housed in two stone-built mills, the earlier one built in 1789. Equipment on display includes an 18 foot diameter waterwheel used to work fulling stocks which "finished" woollen cloth (as produced by hand in a domestic industry). The cotton industry is represented by a spinning room and displays of early machinery. A shop and cafe are included, and there are regular visiting displays. The museum is open to the public (admission charge) each afternoon (except Saturday) from late March to the end of October, but the site is usually "manned" for enquiries etc. at other times. (The car park is free and always open.)

Distance: 5.1km (just over 3 miles) with a number of short climbs, totalling perhaps 65 metres (210ft) of ascent.

Map: Explorer 19 "West Pennine Moors", alternatively Pathfinder 689 "Blackburn".

By car: The museum has a large car park by the B6235 (see inset map).

By public transport: The start can be reached by buses from Rawtenstall bus station (via Haslingden).

This walk again includes part of the East Lancashire Railway's Accrington Extension, this time on the comparatively gentle ascent from the South to the top of Baxenden Bank (for details see Walk 7). Helmshore station, whose site is visited, remained open until the closure of the whole line in 1966. This stretch of line saw one of the worst railway accidents in the North West. In 1860 a series of three Lancashire and Yorkshire excursion trains were returning to Burnley and Colne. Twelve carriages of the second train broke loose crossing Grane Road and ran away back down the line. They collided with the third train near Helmshore station, causing eleven deaths and over sixty injured passengers.

An Edwardian scene at Helmshore station, looking towards Bury. *(J. Ryan collection)*

The Walk

Facing away from the museum, leave the car park by the path in the far left corner. Go through the kissing-gate and left up the stone steps onto the railway. Over to the left, the imposing Tor Hill rises above the former Park Mill. Continuing along the track with the museum below, at a gate there are views across the mill yard to the detached mill chimney high on the hillside above. The track curves right, on a viaduct above the mill lodges (ponds) separated by the River Ogden. To the right, amongst the trees, is the 18th-century Mill Master's House. 100 metres past a further gate, the path drops down from the embankment as the bridge over the Ogden has been demolished. Descend to the footbridge, then bear left to the gate just past a clump of hawthorn bushes and right to regain the rail route. Now it is a straightforward stroll along the embankment towards Haslingden. As Holden Mill approaches on the right, the path descends after a gate to reach a tarmac road. Follow this to reach the B6232 (Grane Road) just where the railway crossed, originally by a tubular iron bridge, which saw the start of the 1860 tragedy. That bridge was removed in 1881 and only the abutments of its replacement are left.

Turn left up the busy B-road past the typical mill workers' housing of Vine Terrace, 1861, and Holden Terrace, 1869, and the former school. By the Holden Arms, cross the B6235 (to Bury) and into a paved lane sign-posted "Holden Wood Reservoir ¼". To the right is the fine St. Stephen's Church, now an antiques centre. Its history includes not only a change of use but also a change of location as it was originally built over a mile further up the Grane valley in 1888. Thirty-eight years later, as the valley became depopulated, it was moved stone by stone to its present site.

Carry on down the lane. After 100 metres, look left across the B-road to see an embankment with a stone wall on its right and cream-coloured factory to the left. This is the route of the quarry tramway from Musbury Heights to the railway section just walked. It crossed this lane just before the reservoir dam, but no real trace remains here. Cross the dam of Holden Wood Reservoir, the oldest (completed 1841) of the three Grane reservoirs which eventually led to the depopulation of the valley. Once over the spillway, cut back left up the hillside to cross a wooden footbridge. Continue with the fence to the right, before dropping steeply down to a stile onto the B6235.

Turn right and walk along the B-road for 150 metres until housing appears on the right. Take the track behind the houses (sign-posted "Musbury Heights"), and climb up the hillside and over two stiles. By the second one, there is a splendid view down to the stretch of railway already walked. Keep on the track as it swings right past the abandoned Lower Park House farm and barn, to cross two stiles. To left and right are typical old "West Pennine" stone buildings. Carry on left down the lane to eventually reach housing and the extensive car parks of Rossendale's most famous successor to the cotton and footwear firms – package holiday giant "Airtours". This is by the B6235 which leads left back to the museum.

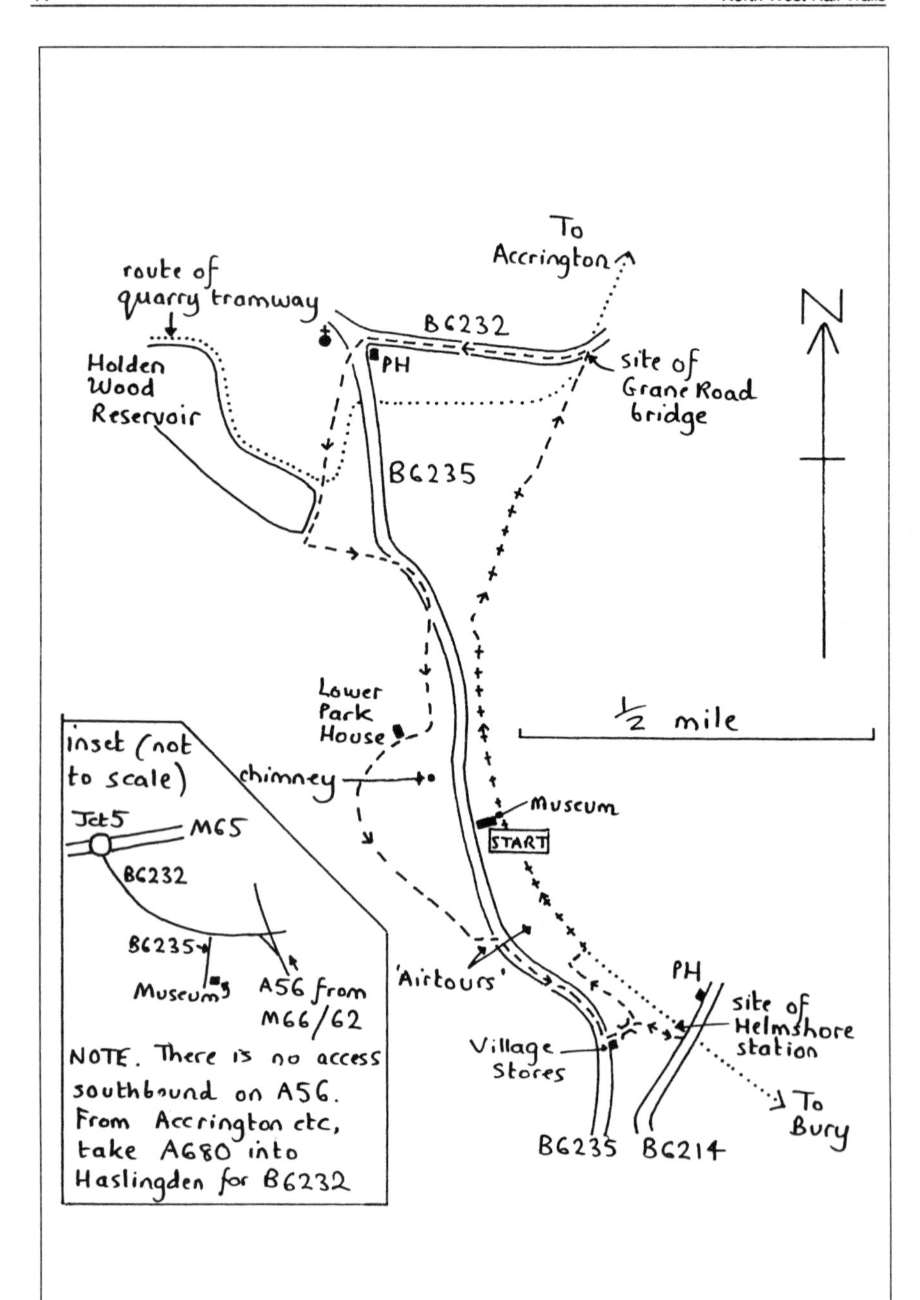
To
Accrington
route of
quarry tramway
B6232
Holden
Wood
Reservoir
PH
site of
Grane Road
bridge
B6235
Lower
Park
House
1/2 mile
inset (not
to scale)
chimney
Museum
START
Jct5
M65
B6232
B6235
Museum
A56 from
M66/62
NOTE. There is no access
southbound on A56.
From Accrington etc,
take A680 into
Haslingden for B6232
'Airtours'
PH
site of
Helmshore
station
Village
Stores
To
Bury
B6235
B6214

For the full walk, turn right instead along the B-road for 350 metres. As the road swings right, by the Village Stores and bus stops, stone steps lead down left to a bridge over the River Ogden. Crossing this, the view towards the church spire shows, below the mill, the stone embankment wall of the former Helmshore station. Straight ahead from the bridge, by old stone-built houses, a tarmac path leads up to the former level crossing on the B6214. This was the only one on the Accrington Extension and remained a bottleneck right up to the line's closure in 1966. Over the road, by "The Stationmaster's House" and a version of a signal box, the track heads away under a bridge. Back across the road, modern bungalows (including "The Sidings"!) occupy the station site. Up the road on the left, just before the Station pub with its colourful sign, was the goods yard, once with three sidings.

Retrace the route back almost to the bridge over the river, but this time take the entry road for the new housing estate. After 60 metres, a gate on the left gives access to a path between the new houses and the river, with unusually tall backs of houses beyond. Follow the path round, past a weir, and up onto the railway embankment, which leads back to the museum's car park.

9. Railways past and present

Irwell Vale

Two lengths of former East Lancashire Railway, once both closed but one now re-opened through the efforts of a preservation society, share this particularly attractive stretch of the Irwell Valley.

Start: Irwell Vale station on the re-opened line to Rawtenstall. GR 793202.

Distance: Two versions of the walk are given – 4.9km (3 miles) on mostly level terrain, or 6.6km (just over 4 miles) with 33 metres (100 feet) of climb. Note that both have a short, steep and sometimes-slippery climb onto the disused railway; the stretches by the Irwell can also be muddy at times.

Map: Explorer 19 "West Pennine Moors", alternatively Pathfinders 700 "Bolton (North) and Horwich" and 689 "Blackburn".

By car: Irwell Vale is reached by a lane from the B6527 at Ewood Bridge, between the A56 at Haslingden and the northern end of the M66 at Edenfield (see inset map). Turn left in the village and follow the lane down to the car park at the station.

By public transport: There is of course a train service to Irwell Vale from Bury and Rawtenstall (Saturdays, Sundays and Bank Holiday Mondays only) also buses from Haslingden and Rawtenstall.

The disused railway section of this route was the southernmost portion of the East Lancashire Railway's Accrington Extension. Opened in 1848, this section climbed steadily on its way to Baxenden Summit (see Walks 7 and 8). It was notable for its bridges, starting with a six span timber viaduct over the Irwell at Alderbottom (replaced with a steel girder bridge in 1881). Next came a nine-arch stone viaduct at Lumb, again over the Irwell, and further north (beyond this walk) a three span stone viaduct over the River Ogden. There were no stations on this stretch, Stubbins having platforms only for the

A summer Sunday steam train on the restored East Lancashire Railway at Strongstry. *(Gordon Suggitt)*

line to Rawtenstall and Bacup. The whole Accrington Extension closed in 1966 and the section walked is now a nature reserve.

The restored line, now re-titled as the East Lancashire Railway, was initially opened by the original ELR in 1846 as far as Rawtenstall, and to Bacup in 1852. It similarly closed in stages, with all services beyond Rawtenstall also ending in 1966. Passenger services to Rawtenstall lasted another six years, but a weekly coal train continued until 1980. The line was re-opened to Ramsbottom by the preservation society in 1987, followed by services to Rawtenstall four years later. Now passenger services operate from Bury each weekend using both steam and diesel. There are intermediate stations at Summerseat and Irwell Vale, and the latter part of this walk is certainly enhanced by activity on the restored line, especially when a "celebrity" steam locomotive is in action. (The East Lancashire Railway at 0161 764 7790 can provide details.)

Irwell Vale is not an original station site, as this was at Ewood Bridge, a half-mile further NE. The new station was opened in 1989, close to the village of Irwell Vale. This was built as an industrial village in the first half of the 19th century and was designated a conservation area in the 1970s, although its original mill was demolished around that time. The village of terraced streets makes an interesting contrast to Lumb, a half-mile to the south. This was an agricultural settlement, with its farmhouse, now the Manor House, and the Old Hall, probably the oldest building remaining in Rossendale. It dates from 1482 and there had been buildings on the site two centuries earlier. Now Lumb is residential with attractive gardens and conversions of farm buildings.

The Walk

From the station, walk back into Irwell Vale, forking right to cross the river. At the crossroads in the centre of the settlement, turn left noting the 1833 date stone on the house at the corner. Walk along Bowker Street, and pass between the Methodist church on the left and the white gable end on Milne Street to the right. By the end of the church, go through a gap in the wall on the right to pick up a footpath leading down to the river. Here cross a footbridge over a stream on the right and walk alongside the Irwell. This stretch can be muddy but there are boards over the worst patches. Pass a weir and sluice gates in the bank to reach the tarmac access road into Lumb.

The route heads left on the road, but it is worth heading right instead – first to admire Lumb Viaduct (no access) then to take a look at the settlement of Lumb. Several of its buildings such as Lower Calf Cote and Lumb Grange are attractive conversions of the farm outbuildings, while further up and to the left are Lumb Manor House (formerly the farm) and Lumb Old Hall. Above these are the very different flats built in the late 1940s to replace old cottages, and originally intended for refugees from Eastern Europe.

If Lumb has been visited, the route must be retraced back down the tarmac access road, past the end of the path from Irwell Vale and over the Irwell. Once over the river, turn right to walk alongside the river with views over to Lumb Viaduct. As a pipe crosses the river, there is a subway left under the restored railway. Ignore this, and instead scramble up the steep and sometimes slippery bank on the right. This leads to the disused railway just to the south of the viaduct, which is fenced off. Head left towards Stubbins on a very overgrown stretch (although the path is clear), this is a Nature Area where new growth has been encouraged. The track is on a massive embankment between the restored railway on the left and the Irwell to the right, which ends at the rusted iron Alderbottom bridge over the river. There are views left to the restored railway's much lower bridge over the river, particularly at the start of the disused bridge. Continue along the trackbed, which now follows a straight course through a shallow cutting, with an attractive moss and fern cover for the wall on the right. Soon after the cutting ends, the track starts to bend left to fencing which marks the limit of public access. Before this, a gate leads into a lane on the right, where there is a choice of routes.

Shorter route to Strongstry: Go left along the lane and left again to pass under the disused railway, then past North View (terrace) and South Terrace with a gabled frontage facing the railway. Go under the second railway bridge (for the restored railway) to arrive by Strongstry Bridge (house).

Longer route to Strongstry: Turn right and follow the track as it bends left past a barn and house to the left. This leads up by the side of a wall on the left, beyond which is a stream in a deep wooded cleft. The gradient eases and the stream now runs alongside the track as it reaches a fence, stile and National Trust sign. Do **not** cross the stile, but instead go left over the stream on a plank footbridge onto a path leading onto the hillside. Here there are fine views across the Irwell valley, before the path passes behind the mansion called "The Cliffe" on the left. This was one of the houses of the Porritt family, owners of the late 19th-century Stubbins Vale Mill, and is now a nursing home. (It was Colonel Porritt who gave land to the National Trust in memory of his son killed at Dunkirk in 1940). The path continues below a high stone wall to the left with a pond on the right, then gently descends through woodland with the zigzag roofs of Stubbins Vale Mill visible through the trees. Next on the right is a strange folly-like structure. This is the "Wet Tower", apparently used in the production of cloth at the mill below. Continue on the stoney track past the base of the mill's chimney to reach stone-built housing. Walk along the terrace (East View) and straight on towards

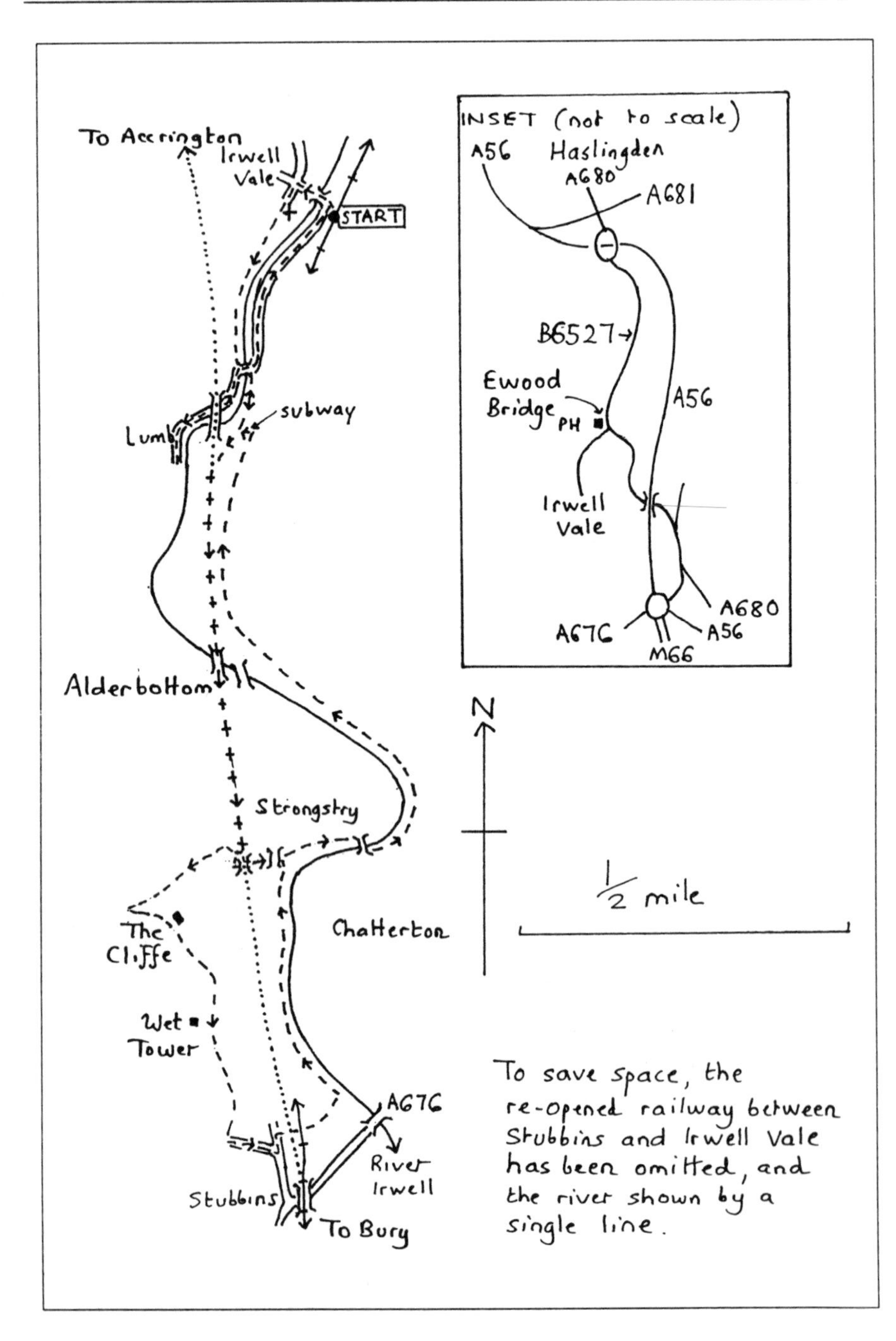
INSET (not to scale)
A56
Haslingden
A680
A681
B6527
Ewood Bridge
PH
Irwell Vale
A56
A680
A676
A56
M66
To Accrington
Irwell Vale
START
Lumb
subway
Alderbottom
Strongstry
The Cliffe
Chatterton
Wet Tower
A676
River Irwell
Stubbins
To Bury
N
1/2 mile
To save space, the re-opened railway between Stubbins and Irwell Vale has been omitted, and the river shown by a single line.

a metal gate. Turn left here on a paved road past housing and industry. By the "Gate no. 7" sign, turn left at the Public Footpath sign to follow the tarmac towards the mills. Within 35 metres there is a car parking area on the right. This is over the disused railway route and would be the car park for the proposed Stubbins halt on the restored railway just beyond the fence.

Immediately after the car park, turn right through the rather insalubrious subway beneath both railways (this is also scheduled for improvement as part of the preservation railway's plans) noting the steps up to the right which once led to the platforms of Stubbins station. Continue towards the brick-built mill at Chatterton, past housing on the right, to reach the Irwell. Turn left through a metal gate to follow the river upstream. There are unusually gabled cottages on the left before the path bears left towards the railway bridge. Turn right on the lane to pass Strongstry Bridge (house).

Return from Strongstry (both routes): Continue past the strangely uniform terraces of Strongstry village on the left to reach the bridge over the river. Cross this and immediately turn left through the gate into the meadow by the riverside. This is a particularly attractive stretch of river scenery although it can be muddy after wet weather. Go over a stile and pass the sculptures – part of the Irwell Sculpture Trail. The path now bears away from the river bend with glimpses of the two Alderbottom railway bridges on the left. Keep on the path over a stile and across a track and tiny stream, before the restored railway is reached. The route now follows this railway until the valley opens out with views ahead to Irwell Vale station. To reach this it is necessary to use the underpass noted on the outward journey, reached on the left. After it, turn right to walk alongside the Irwell, first on a path, then after the road bridge leading to Lumb, on a road with new housing on the right. A right turn as the settlement is reached leads back to the station car park.

10. Past electrics, present steam

Tottington

Electric trains to Holcombe Brook are long gone but steam trains have returned on the line to Ramsbottom, at least at weekends. Both lines are visited on this walk which starts at a site from industrial history, now a country park.

Start: Burrs Country Park, north of Bury. GR 798126.

Distance: 7.9km (just under 5 miles), on mostly level terrain though with a few short sharp climbs. There can be a few muddy patches, especially close by the River Irwell towards the end of the walk.

Map: Explorer 19 "West Pennine Moors", alternatively Pathfinder 700 "Bolton (North) and Horwich".

By car: The start can be reached from the B6214 road, which links Bury to Ramsbottom via Holcombe Brook. Coming from Bury, it is sign-posted "Burrs Country Park" to the right, 300 yards after the B6214 has diverged from the B6213 Tottington Road. From the north, it can be reached by Hunstanton Drive which is a left turn almost a mile after the start of the built-up area of Bury. It has had a "Burrs Country Park" sign but this has been missing at times. However, a "Bury Town Centre" cycleway sign and the Woodbank Surgery Medical Centre identify the left turn (see inset map). From either direction, proceed through the housing areas to the start of the country park. At the "Burrs" sign and distinctive sculpture of birds on a waterwheel (part of the Irwell Sculpture Trail), carry on left on a quite long stretch of cobbled lane to reach Burrs proper. Immediately after the bridge over the Irwell, turn left into the large car park, just below the mill chimney.

By public transport: There is no bus service to Burrs; the nearest bus stops are those at the end of Hunstanton Drive for services between Bury Interchange and Ramsbottom/Edenfield, but this adds another kilometre to the total distance. An alternative would be to use the same service to the Old Duke pub on the B6214 and start/finish the walk there.

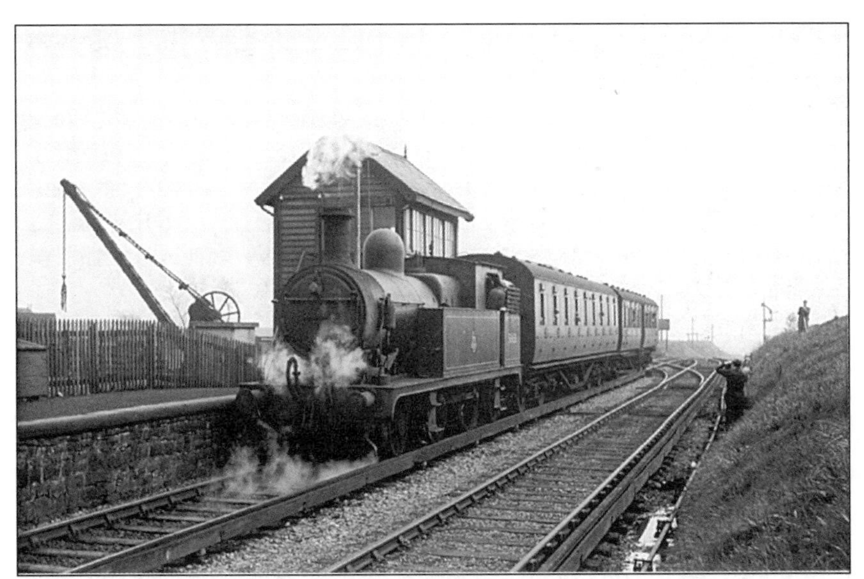

Steam traction returned to the Holcombe Brook branch (after 38 years of electric trains) as shown by this Bury-bound train in the last month of passenger services – May 1952. *(Author's collection)*

The Holcombe Brook line was built independently, but was operated by the Lancashire and Yorkshire Railway from its start in 1882 and absorbed by it six years later. Its claim to fame is that it was powered by electric traction for about half of its working life. This began with an experimental overhead scheme in 1913, replaced by third-rail operation after five years. This lasted until 1951 when steam took over for the last years of the line. Passenger services ended in 1952, followed by a cutback in freight from Holcombe Brook to Tottington in 1960 and complete closure three years later. From the start, the railway suffered from competition on the nearby roads, which accounts for the profusion of passenger stops. Between the start at Bury (Bolton Street) and Holcombe Brook, four miles away, there were three intermediate stations (Woolfold, Tottington and Greenmount), and four halts were also opened. Now nothing remains except the trackbed between Woolfold and Greenmount, plus the viaducts at Tottington and Woodhill. The former is included on this walk, but the latter, a fine six-span structure over the Irwell, can be reached from 500 metres along Woodhill Road in the opposite direction to Burrs (see inset map). Follow the cycle path 200 metres to the viaduct (GR 801117).

Details of the restored East Lancashire Railway are given in Walk 9. While it provides interest for the final leg of the walk at weekends, there is no direct access as a planned halt at Burrs has not yet been provided. (The station at Summerseat is only just beyond the walk's northernmost point and could therefore be used as start and finish of a version of the walk.)

Burrs Country Park is based around the remains of a late 18th-century industrial settlement built for cotton-spinning and originally using water power from the River Irwell. By the mid-19th century, it was converted to steam power before becoming a bleach works and eventually closing in 1933. The site fell into neglect, many of its buildings being demolished in 1952, before it was made into a country park in 1987. Now the mill site, overlooked by its chimney of 1850, has been excavated to reveal extensive foundations and watercourses. The stone back-to-back cottages have been rebuilt, and provide an information point and activity centre (mostly for water sports especially canoeing), while the nearby Brown Cow still functions as a pub (although it was built as a farmhouse in 1752, and thus predates the area's industrial activity).

The Walk

From the car park, walk back over the Irwell and once across the bridge, turn right up steps to cross the canal feeder. This, which has just crossed the Irwell on an imposing aqueduct, sent water three miles to Elton Reservoir south of Bury. This was built in 1805 as the main source for the Bury branch of the Manchester, Bolton and Bury Canal (see Walk 21 for more on this canal). Past the feeder, continue up the steps and at the top, bear right to keep housing on the left and views over Burrs and towards Holcombe Tower to the right. Eventually the path swings left round the end of the housing to reach the B6214 at a dental surgery. Turn right on the B-road to pass the Old Duke pub, then cross the road and head left into Garside Hey Road. At the bottom of this road, by a public footpath sign, head slightly left across the field. Soon the embankment of the Holcombe Brook branch appears straight ahead across a small steep-sided valley. Descend to a concrete footbridge just past an overgrown goit (mill channel). Although it is possible to head left to roughly where Woolfold station stood, garden areas have encroached onto the trackbed and no traces remain. Instead head over the footbridge and straight up the slope to the railway.

Turn right along the abandoned trackbed with views of the moors above Holcombe and Edenfield. Soon, after crossing a small valley, the track enters quite a lengthy cutting ending at a deeper valley. The halt at Sunnywood was hereabouts, but nothing remains. Nor is anything left at the site of Tottington station 400 metres further on, past the playing fields and school. The only reminders of the railway, apart from the trackbed, come soon after this. First a stone bridge crosses the line, then there is the viaduct over the very edge of a mill lodge (reservoir). This is best seen by taking the path down on the right 50 metres from the far end of the viaduct to reach the banks of the lodge. It is possible to return to the trackbed and walk another 700 metres along it, past the sites of the halt at Knowles and station at Greenmount (both without any remains) to reach Brandlesholme Road (B6215). From here on, the last 800 metres of the line into Holcombe Brook have been lost completely to housing developments. (If this is walked, the route of the main walk can be rejoined by turning right and walking along the road for 700 metres, watching out for the lane from Tower Farm – see map.)

The suggested route continues along the main track slightly away from the north side of the lodge as it swings left to the aptly named Tower Farm. Walk under its "battlements" and then turn right towards cottages and on to the B6215. Turn right and in 75 metres at a "Public Footpath" sign, go left through the hedge and over to a footbridge. Bear left from this up to the B6214, which is crossed to the footpath heading right (*not* the track going left). Follow the tall hedge on the left round a bend to a fence with a stile. Cross this and walk alongside the electric fence. Despite the pylons, there are good views left to Scout Moor and Knowl Hill. At the end of the field, cross another stile into a lane where views extend down the Irwell valley and (if clear) away to the Pennines. Go down the roughly surfaced lane to the quite extensive and in some cases attractive buildings of Wood Road.

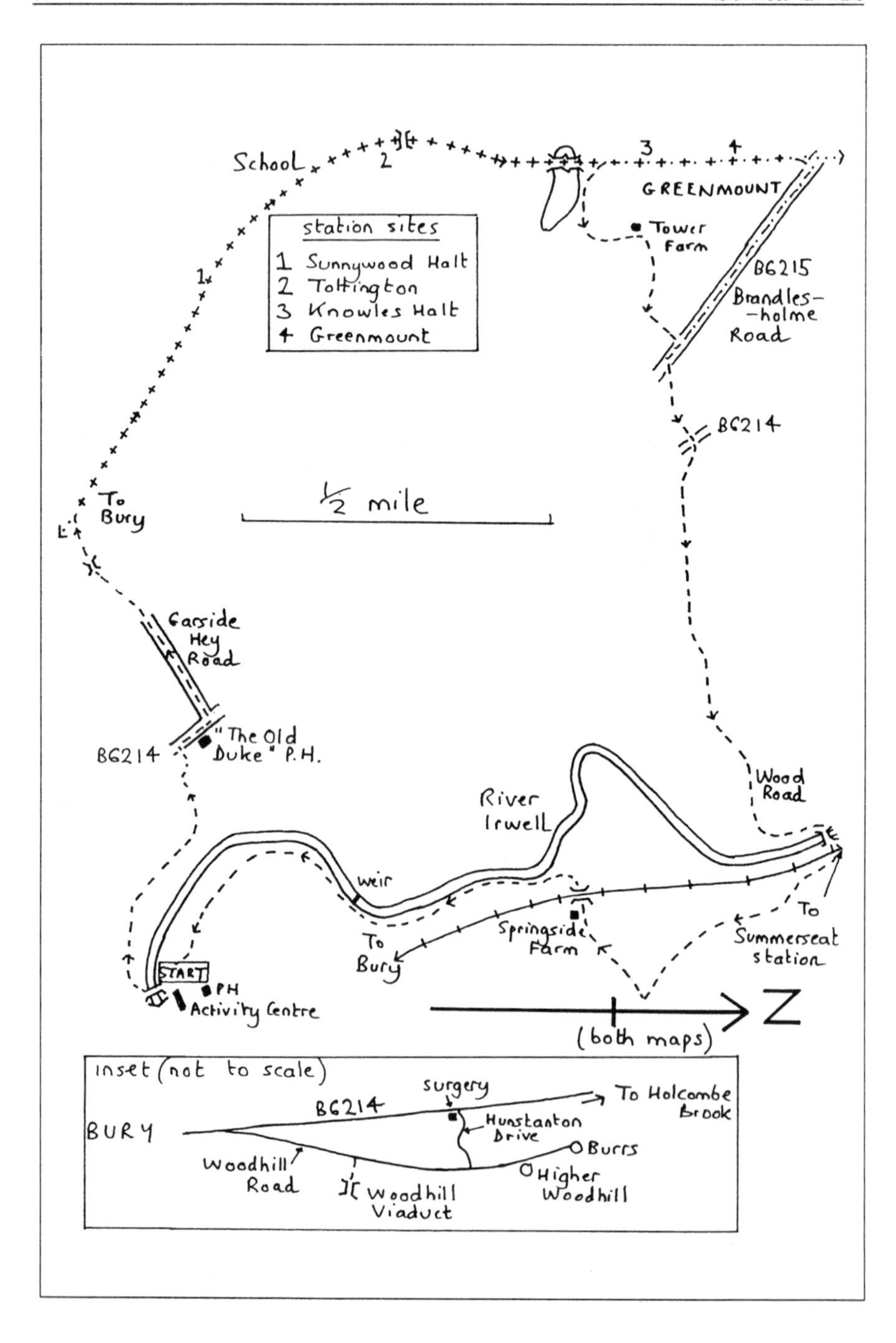

School
1
2
3
4
GREENMOUNT
station sites
1 Sunnywood Halt
2 Tottington
3 Knowles Halt
4 Greenmount
Tower Farm
B6215
Brandles-holme Road
B6214
To Bury
½ mile
Garside Hey Road
"The Old Duke" P.H.
B6214
River Irwell
Wood Road
weir
To Bury
Springside Farm
To Summerseat station
START
PH
Activity Centre
N
(both maps)
inset (not to scale)
surgery
B6214
To Holcombe Brook
BURY
Hunstanton Drive
Burrs
Woodhill Road
Higher Woodhill
Woodhill Viaduct

Follow the lane through the settlement to the bridge over the Irwell. Across this, take the stone steps straight ahead (with an Irwell Valley Way sign) to cross the railway with care. Summerseat station is just visible 350 metres up the line. Continue on the path up and away from the railway to a stile at a junction, where a right turn above the railway is taken. Cross a boardway between kissing gates to reach a grassy shelf above a sizeable pond usually with birdlife. Go through a further gate onto a stoney path leading eventually to a tarmac lane. Turn right onto the lane and pass a surprising collection of cut stone on the right to reach Springside Farm. Keep on the lane to pass the farm buildings on the left, and go under the bridge of the preserved railway.

Immediately past the bridge, go left over a stile and onto a path which keeps high above a stream to the right as the Irwell comes into view. The path swings left between fences with the railway over on the left. Keep on the path as it leaves the fences at a stile and bears left above the river which is strangely still along this stretch. The reason for this is usually heard before it is seen, as the path drops down steps to the bank just above a magnificent weir holding back the river. The route now follows a clear path alongside the channel from the weir to Burrs, with the earth ramparts of the ancient Castlesteads camp over to the left. The path reaches Burrs at a "stone circle" (another part of the Irwell Sculpture Trail), with a former sluice gate over on the right. This leads to the canal feeder, which can be followed to steps down to the car park. Alternatively, the path can be continued past a pond on the left (used for watersports), past an information board for the site and down to the activity centre before returning to the start.

11. Tunnels and tramways

Stacksteads

There are enough remains of the railway and quarry tramways in Rossendale's "the Valley" to make a fascinating puzzle to unravel on this walk.

Start: The centre of Stacksteads at GR 854218.

Distance: 6.2km (almost 4 miles) with 60 metres (195 feet) of climb.

Map: Outdoor Leisure 21 "South Pennines".

By car: Park in the car park in the centre of Stacksteads, on the north side of the A681 Rawtenstall-Bacup road.

By public transport: There are frequent Accrington to Rochdale buses along the A681 through Stacksteads, although some services from Rochdale require a change of bus in Bacup.

The original East Lancashire Railway encountered in Walks 9, 10 and 21 terminated in 1846 at Rawtenstall. It was extended to Newchurch two years later and to Bacup in 1852. The extension was built as a single track, but doubled by 1881. This caused particular problems in the narrow valley of the Irwell east of Newchurch. The single line had used two tunnels through this obstacle, but the doubling necessitated a completely new bore, parallel to the two original tunnels; this single tunnel was known by the expressive name of the "Thrutch". Between Rawtenstall and Bacup, there were intermediate stations at Clough Fold, Newchurch (re-named Waterfoot in 1881) and Stacksteads. Both goods trains and passenger services (to Bury, with some trains continuing through to Manchester) continued to be well-used until the 1950s, but then fell away steadily despite the early introduction of diesel multiple units in 1956. The line was singled east of Stacksteads in 1960 and closed completely beyond Rawtenstall six years later.

Time has not dealt kindly with the former Rawtenstall-Bacup line. Its first half-mile has disappeared under the A681 as it bypasses

An ex-Lancashire and Yorkshire loco pulls a passenger train from Bury into Bacup in 1953. *(J Davenport)*

Rawtwenstall and much of the rest of the trackbed has gone for builders' yards, factory car parks etc. Most of its tunnels are sealed up, its many bridges over the Irwell demolished and its stations gone completely. However its main remaining walkable stretch, the scanty remains of a station, some bridge piers and one walkable tunnel are all included on this walk. The only other walkable length is about half a mile from Clough Fold towards Waterfoot, although this does include the best remaining bridge over the Irwell at GR 825222.

The story of Rossendale's tramways for the stone-quarrying industry is far too complex to cover here. Basically in the second half of the 19th century, "Haslingden Flagstone" was extensively quarried (and in some cases mined) for pavements throughout the northern industrial towns. Here quarries dug into the steep southern side of the Irwell valley were able to use tramways down to the railway in the valley bottom below. These used inclines often worked by stationary engines, but with conventional loco haulage in the quarries and on more level moorland stretches above, and in the sidings below. In the area walked, quarrying in this way seems to have finished around the outbreak of the First World War, but many of the inclines and mineral line routes can still be traced on the ground.

The Walk

Leaving the Bacup end of the car park, cross the road to go down a lane between Acre Mill Carpets and the Rose'n'Bowl restaurant/bar (sign-posted "Stacksteads Recreation Ground"). Cross the culverted stream and go immediately right through a gate to the River Irwell. The former railway is up on the right on a landscaped embankment, but follow the path to a blue-painted bridge over the river. This marks the crossing point for a tramway built by Richard Siddall, which can be seen heading up an incline on the hillside to the left. On the right it led into sidings by the railway, now lost to landscaping. Cross the bridge and turn right to follow the left bank of the Irwell. At the road, go left for less than 50 metres which gives a view down to the rusting remains of the railway bridge which once supported Stacksteads station. Turn back along the road and down towards the Railway Tavern. The scruffy ground behind the buildings has the overgrown end of the station platform (Stacksteads, like Clough Fold and Bacup, had an island platform), and the road crosses the site of a level crossing.

At the main road by the parish church, turn left noting the attractive tiling at the entrances to the first row of shops. Go down the next left (Siding Street) and turn right at the end. The landscaped area now on the left marks the rail route just after the western end of Stacksteads' platform, and from here on the line was accompanied by private sidings for some distance, especially on the up (southern) side. Go along the street parallel to the former railway, with first housing on the right, then the four-storey Rossendale Mill (1860). Just past the mill's stone chimney, a gate on the left overlooking the

Irwell leads up onto the embankment, where a path leading diagonally downhill from the left follows the incline of a tramway from Brandwood quarry.

Turn right to follow the railway along its main surviving stretch, above first the Irwell, then a cricket pitch, with a temporary break as the path crosses a road with a rusty metal bridge over the filled-in railway. After the road, the path returns to the railway and follows it to the tunnels which gave such problems during the line's construction. On the left, the later single Thrutch tunnel is blocked off, but the right-hand Newchurch No. 2 tunnel is still fully walkable. At 265 metres it is quite a length, and can be quite eerie as water drips from the ceiling, nearby road traffic roars by and the only light is at the end of the proverbial tunnel! At the far end, the path emerges into a gorge-like section of the Irwell valley (known locally as the Glen) with the shorter No. 1 tunnel ahead blocked-off, so that the path soon heads for the busy A681. Luckily this has a pavement which can be followed past Glen Terrace to the road left marked "Hugh Business Park". Turn left into this and cross the Irwell. At the first cottages on the left, head left on a stoney path uphill to a point just above the blocked-in western entrances of the tunnels. Here there is a good view over the line as it continued west through the present coal yard and to the left of the church spire at Waterfoot.

The path continues up above the houses just passed on the main road and round to a small quarry on the right. From here there are splendid views over the gorge and tunnels, plus a panorama in the other direction towards Rawtenstall. Ignore the path clinging to the top of the gorge and instead bear right through a gateway and over a stile onto the football pitches. Cross these diagonally to a stone stile in the opposite corner by some green cabins. Over the stile, turn left into a roughly surfaced lane and pass Heys Farm and stone-built houses and farms to reach a tarmac road at the settlement of Rake Head.

Turn right on the tarmac and left at a junction to pass beneath Brandwood Quarry, now used for waste disposal but mercifully hidden by tree-planting. Heavy trucks use this section of road but after the first of several stone terraces on the left, turn right at a postbox where the tramway from Brandwood Quarry crossed en route for the

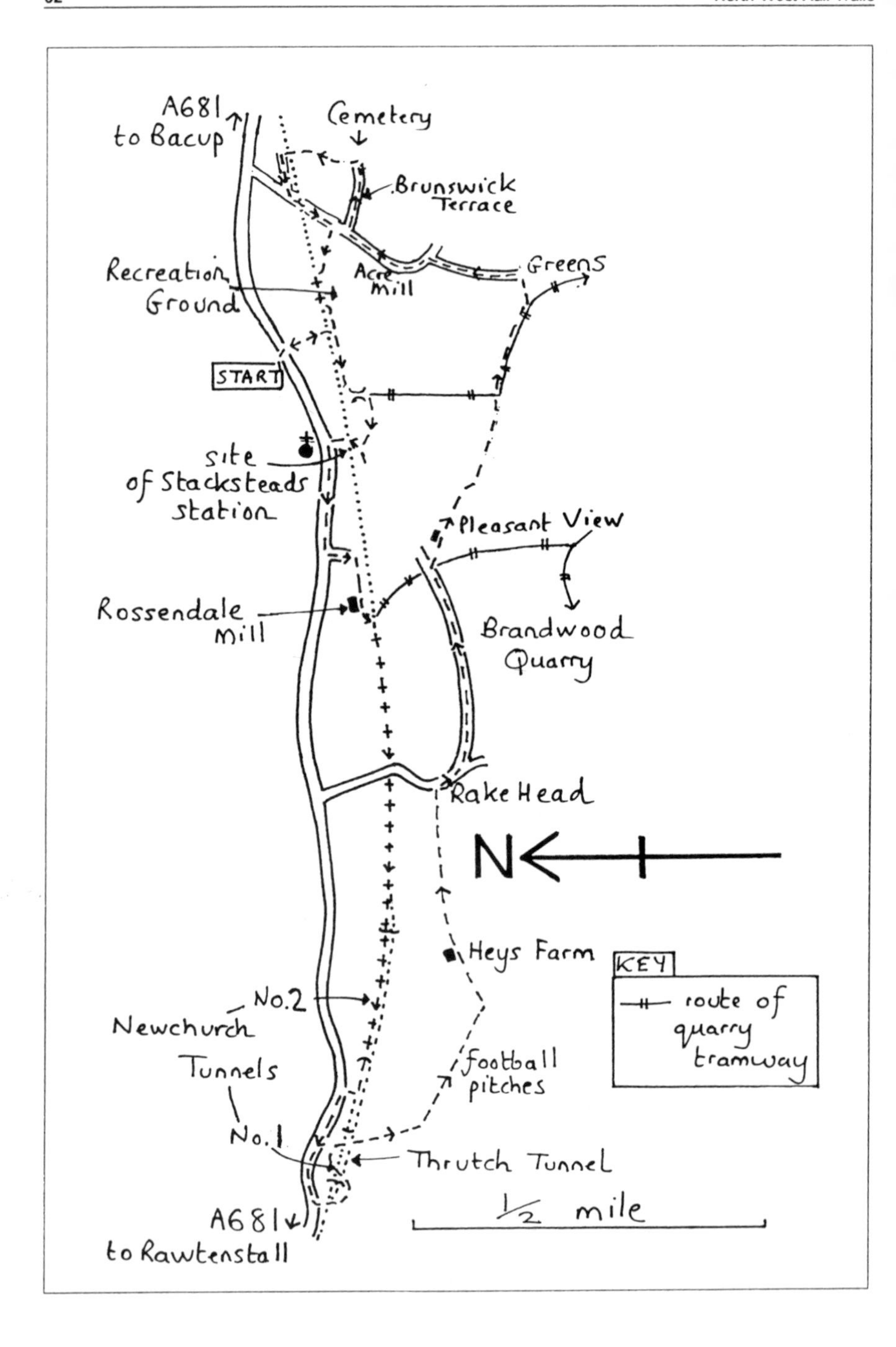
A681 to Bacup
Cemetery
Brunswick Terrace
Greens
Recreation Ground
Acre Mill
START
site of Stacksteads station
Pleasant View
Rossendale Mill
Brandwood Quarry
Rake Head
N
Heys Farm
KEY
route of quarry tramway
No.2
Newchurch Tunnels
No.1
football pitches
Thrutch Tunnel
½ mile
A681 to Rawtenstall

railway near Rossendale Mill. Head up the track above the former tramway route to pass a higher terrace ("Pleasant View") on the left. Continue on this track to the next cottages, and take the right fork through gates marked "Concessionary Footpath". Ignore the track going right towards the spoil heaps and head left between a wall and a fence. 100 metres after the cottages, the path crosses another clear tramway heading downhill in a shallow cutting. This is Siddall's tramway, previously seen at the blue footbridge near the start of the walk. Despite older routes up by the wall towards the quarry and derelict farm, this tramway's main route led by a complex junction into the track being walked from here on. A little further along, its tramway origin is clear as it forms a distinct embankment above the fields on either side. This ends overlooking a track up the hillside as the hamlet of Greens is reached (although its route continued uphill left of the track). Go left of the end of the embankment and between the first houses of Greens to the tarmac access lane.

Here the tarmac can be followed down into Stacksteads to pass Acre Mill. Just **before** crossing the Irwell, turn right into Brunswick Terrace, which leads to the cemetery gates. Turn left at the cemetery to pass through a gate overlooking a massive mill. The path swings right and down, past cottages, and over the Irwell to the bridge piers of the railway as it crossed both lane and river. Turn left after these into Holme Street, then left again to pass the mill. At the end of the terrace on the right, turn right past Woodhey Engineering (noting that the end of Wardle Street has terraces still occupied as back-to -backs) and into the Recreation Ground. At the right a stretch of cindery embankment is a last indication of the railway, before a right turn at the end of the field into the lane leads back to the starting point.

Note: Anyone wishing to walk more of Rossendale's quarry tramways should refer to Robin Martin's "North West Railway Walks" (Sigma Press, 1990). The book is out of print but copies may be available in local libraries.

12. "New Line" over the summit

Britannia

Contrasting approaches to the use of old railways are in evidence on this walk over the highest point on the former Lancashire and Yorkshire Railway system.

Start: New Line car park and picnic site off the A6060 south east of Bacup. GR 876216.

Distance: 6.5km (just over 4 miles) with 105 metres (340 ft) height gain, mostly on the return climb from Shawforth.

Map: Outdoor Leisure 21 "South Pennines".

By car: The A6060 forms a southern bypass to Bacup, between Stacksteads and Britannia, with the car park close to halfway, on its southern side. It is not well sign-posted and the entrance is easily missed. Coming from the Stacksteads direction, after the entrances to the industrial estates on the left, there is a short stretch of housing along the road. At the end of the terraces, opposite two new bungalows, an insignificant sign points right into the car park. Coming the other way, from Britannia, the road bends right over the former railway bridge, and the two bungalows appear on the right with the entrance opposite them, on the left.

By public transport: Bus services along the A6060 are almost non-existent, but there is a good service along the A671 just to the north, from Accrington, Rawtenstall and Bacup to Rochdale. Alight by the Wellington pub and Britannia post office and start by walking back towards Bacup (see map).

The name "New Line" is still in local use almost 120 years after the railway it refers to opened and over 50 years after its closure for passengers and goods. The link from Rochdale was completed into Bacup in 1881, almost 30 years after the line from Bury and Rawtenstall (see Walk 11). It was built by the Lancashire and Yorkshire Railway only to keep out the Manchester, Sheffield and Lincolnshire Railway, involved considerable engineering difficulties, and soon became a loss-maker as Rochdale trams ran along the nearby road by 1911. Only the section from Facit to Bacup will be dealt with here, as the lower part of the branch is covered in the next walk.

The upper section involved gradients of 1 in 40 from Shawforth up to the summit at Britannia, 967 feet (295 metres) above sea level. This was the highest point on the whole LYR system, higher than its main Pennine crossings further east. After it came an even steeper descent into Bacup at 1 in 34. Intermediate stations were provided at Shawforth and Britannia; both closed in 1917 though Shawforth did later re-open. Goods traffic was initially significant, especially stone from moorland quarries, but once this ended in 1947 the whole branch closed, with one exception. This was the engine shed at Bacup, opened in 1882 to replace an earlier shed on the line to Rawtenstall. In 1921 thirty seven locos were shedded there; by closure in 1954 this was down to eight and their departure to Bury meant the whole line north of Facit went out of use.

The area's former industries are also well shown on this walk, with evidence of cotton, coal and especially stone. The latter is best

The trackbed of the former Bacup-Rochdale line near Britannia.

represented by the remains of the Britannia Quarries system. This was a standard gauge tramway to quarries south of the watershed, towards Whitworth. Operational by the 1880s, it used a self-activating incline down to sidings west of Britannia station. It continued to be worked by rail much later than most Rossendale quarry systems, but when this finished in the 1940s, it contributed to the closure of the railway above Facit.

The Walk

Leave the far end of the car park on a clear path which soon joins the line of the former railway coming in from the filled-in road bridge on the left. Next is a strangely lopsided bridge over the route. Its odd outline is due to it carrying a tramway incline at a steep angle down the hillside from a coal mine down to a cotton mill – all long gone. The path then crosses a stream and follows a craggy cutting towards a pipe and a more conventional bridge. Up to here the climb has been quite steep, but now the gradient eases towards new housing before climbing up to a filled-in bridge. This marks the end of the section most recognisable as a former rail line. In fact all the next 200 metres of railway have been filled in, completely hiding the site of long-closed Britannia station and obscuring the actual summit of the line at the next bridge. Past this, another variant on dealing with old railway lines is found. Here a stretch alongside the A671 has been "tidied up" with a patch of neatly cut grass, ornamental railings, and a pavement by the road. Luckily this soon ends, and a more recogniszable rail route, though still grassed over, heads distinctly downhill below a battlemented gable end high on the valleyside.

The grassy rail route is soon high above the road as it swings right, below a detached mill chimney on the far hillside, towards an amazingly intact original footbridge. Past this, the grassy swathe continues towards modern housing where the former trackbed abruptly ends. Head along the line of bungalows on either side, and after a children's playground on the right, as the road makes a sharp right turn, look out for a cream and brown painted stairway to the left. Descend this, noting the plaque which explains the lack of railway at this point! At the end of the "subway", turn right alongside the former railway's fine stonework and walk along to a sharp right turn back to the line of the railway. Just before more ornamental railings, turn left past garages to regain the trackbed, again grassed over. Head along this through the former Shawforth Quarry, which had a branch from the railway of which no sign remains, the site having been extensively landscaped. Continue towards large spoil heaps of the quarries across the valley. Further to the left the far hillside is dotted with the waste from coal-mining. Cross a farm access road, again with fine stonework, to reach the limit of walkable line on this section at a missing bridge by a group of cottages.

At this point it is necessary to retrace the route back to Shawforth. This time turn left on the tarmac road just past the garages and walk up through the modern housing. Ignore two right turns to keep left past the typical Pennine farmstead of Knott Hill Farm. The road is now a narrow quiet lane which leads uphill to gain fine views over the valley, with the railway hidden deep below, before these are obscured by woodland to the right. Keep on the lane to pass Shore End Cottage and sheds, where the lane becomes a rough track with the battlemented farm clear across the valley. The slope levels off by more woodland on the right and then descends steeply towards Britannia, reaching the railway at the filled-in bridge by the summit. Go through the gateway on the former bridge and this time take the narrower path on the left of the filled-in railway track. As this continues through kissing-gates on either side of a farm track, it is soon above the railway in its cutting, with Britannia's mill and chapel to the right. On the left, a clear stone embankment indicates the line of the Britannia Quarries tramway system as it came to join the railway at the last fllled-in bridge. This soon becomes a siding for road access for taking the stone away over the next bridge, as the main incline disappeared left up the hillside along this stretch. (The incline is not clear across the lower fields but will be seen later.)

Turn right to cross the next bridge over the railway and pass the mill – a rare example of one still working in textiles – then left along the A6060. Take the first right (Cobden Street) to reach the A671 by the Wellington pub. Turn left here and walk along a broad stretch of road until housing finishes on the left. Now looking back across the valley, the Britannia Quarries incline can clearly be seen coming di-

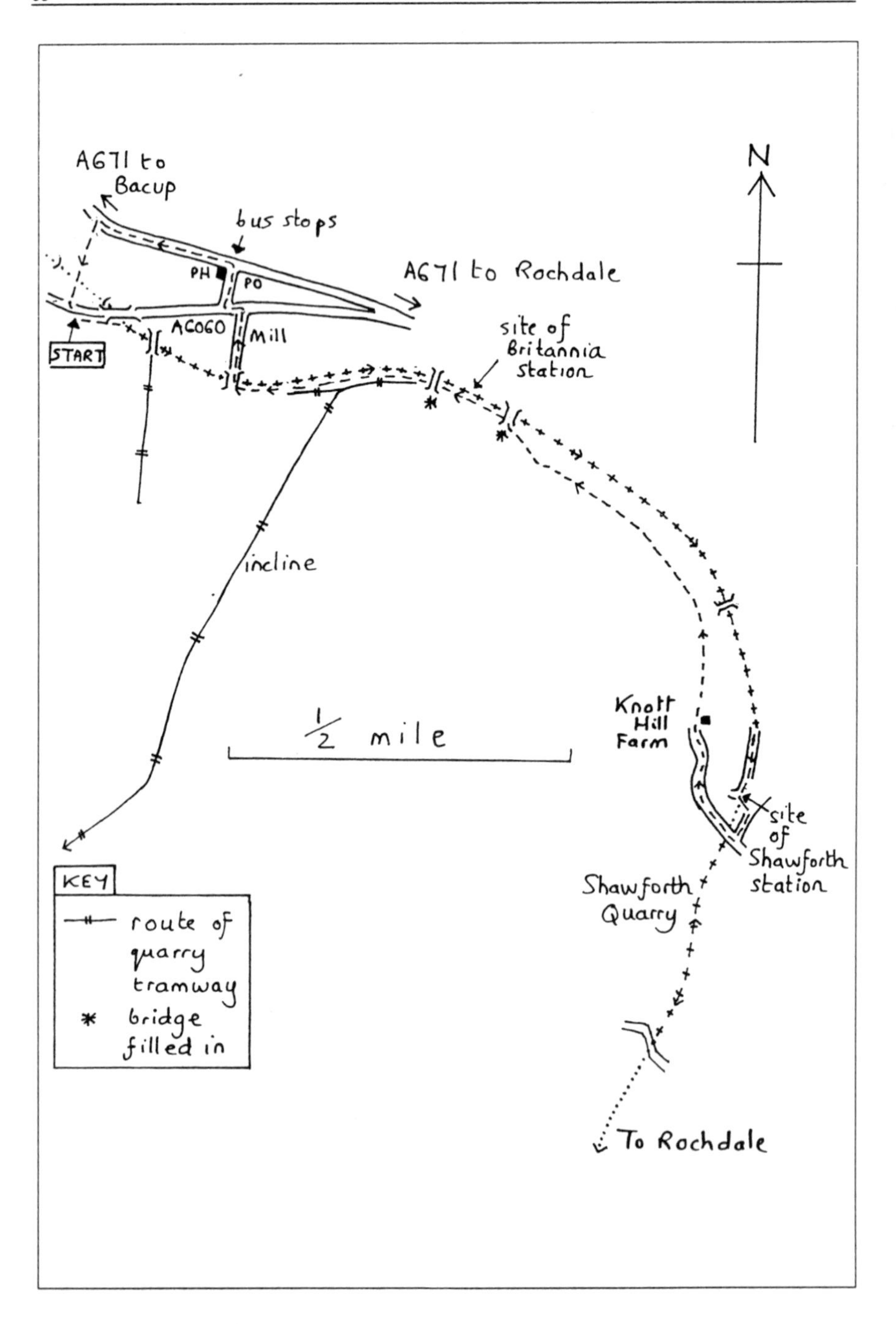

A671 to Bacup
bus stops
A671 to Rochdale
N
PH
PO
A6060
Mill
START
site of Britannia station
incline
1/2 mile
Knott Hill Farm
site of Shawforth station
Shawforth Quarry
KEY
route of quarry tramway
bridge filled in
To Rochdale

agonally downhill, especially where it used an embankment to pass left of the chalet-like building high on the far hillside. A fine view also opens up ahead down the main Rossendale valley. As the road bends past the end of housing to the right, turn left just past the bus shelter onto a rough track leading downhill. Just past the old farm to the left, stop and look over the rusty remains of a gate on the right. Immediately below and out of sight is the west portal of the former Britannia Tunnel. The railway went straight ahead towards low brown industrial units in the middle distance, while the engine shed site is now occupied by a huge blue and grey unit on the right. Continue to the road where the car park entrance is diagonally left. However to see the east portal of the tunnel, turn left up the road for 150 metres to look left at the filled-in and fenced-off entrance before returning to the car park.

13. To the dell

Whitworth

A second walk along the Bacup-Rochdale line is combined here with extensive views and spectacular river scenery, all reached from the historic area of Whitworth Square.

Start: Whitworth village, three miles north of Rochdale on the A671. GR 884177.

Distance: 6km (3¾ miles) with 145 metres (470 ft) height gain, in several climbs.

Map: Outdoor Leisure 21 "South Pennines", alternatively Pathfinder 701 "Bury, Rochdale and Littleborough".

By car: Whitworth is on the A671 which links Rochdale with Bacup and Burnley. There are car parks on the main road (Market Street) close to the start of the walk, the nearest being just south of the Dog and Partridge pub.

By public transport: There are frequent bus services from Rochdale to Bacup, with additional ones as far as Shawforth.

The first section of the line from Rochdale, as far as Facit, was completed by the Lancashire and Yorkshire Railway in 1870 despite major construction difficulties including landslides, gradients as steep as 1 in 50, and the 105 feet high viaduct at Healey Dell. The six mile single track section to Facit was well-provided with stations at Wardleworth, Shawclough, Broadley, Whitworth and Facit. The line was never a commercial success despite stone quarry traffic from several inclines down from the moors to the west. This finished in 1947, the same year as passenger services ended on the whole branch. Goods trains however continued to Facit until 1963 and Whitworth kept a coal train a day until 1967 when the line closed completely. In addition to this walk, this lower section of the branch can be walked for almost another kilometre into a housing area on the outskirts of Rochdale. Little remains of the branch's structures, with the magnificent exception of Healey Dell viaduct.

As well as the rail line, the village of Whitworth is worth studying. Its area of Whitworth Square, visited on the walk, was made a conservation area on account of its rich variety of old buildings, and its connections with the "Whitworth Doctors". About sixteen members of one Whitworth family, the Taylors, practiced medicine during the late 18th and 19th centuries, achieving fame far beyond such a small and remote settlement. Their residence, Whitworth House, and several cottages used as patients' lodgings are seen at the start of the walk.

A rare visitor to the site of Broadley station in 1967, the year the branch closed completely. Normal passenger services had ended 20 years earlier. *(Author's collection)*

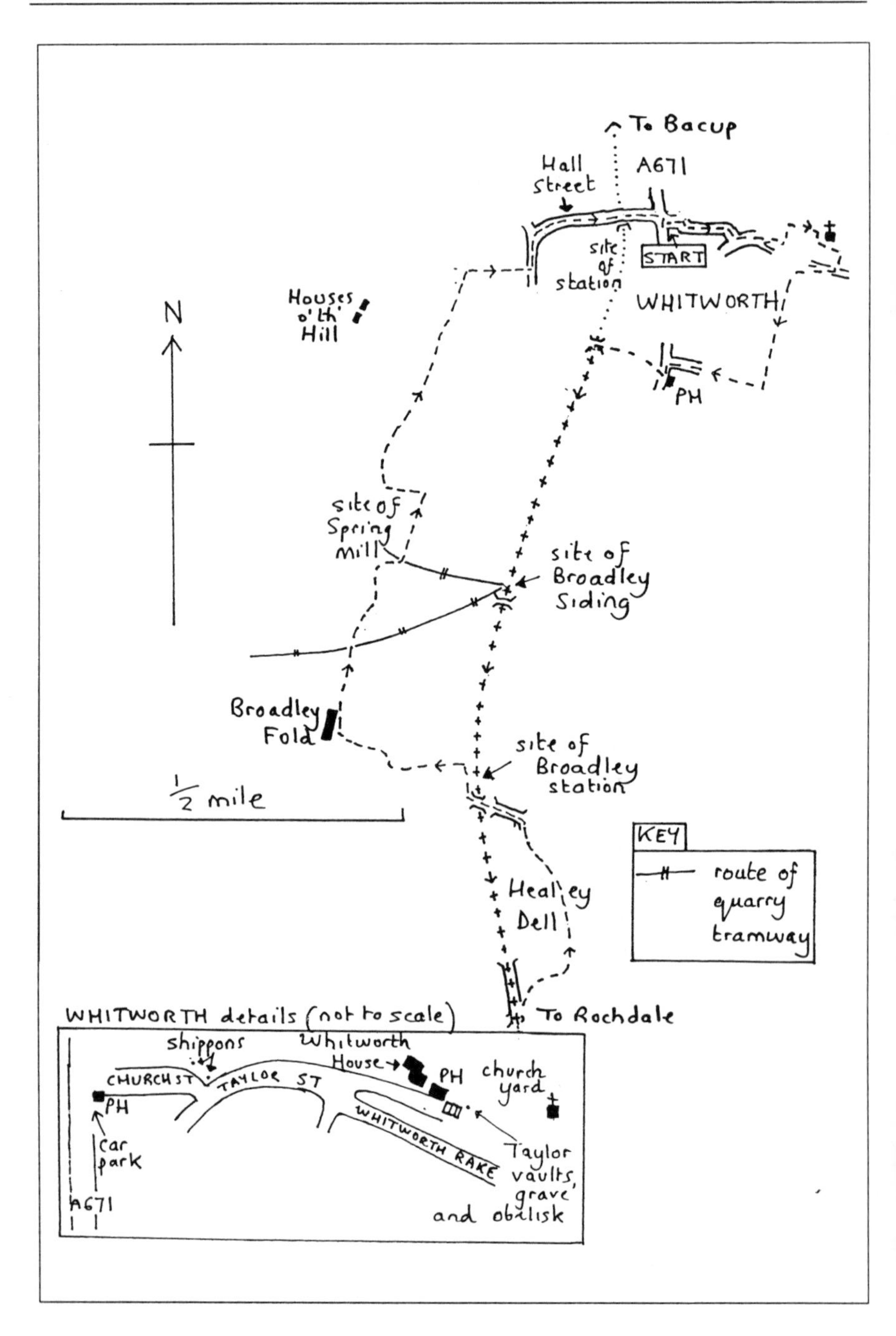
To Bacup
Hall Street
A671
site of station
START
WHITWORTH
Houses o'th' Hill
N
PH
site of Spring mill
site of Broadley Siding
Broadley Fold
site of Broadley station
1/2 mile
KEY
route of quarry tramway
Healey Dell
To Rochdale
WHITWORTH details (not to scale)
shippons
Whitworth House
PH
church yard
CHURCH ST
TAYLOR ST
WHITWORTH RAKE
PH
car park
A671
Taylor vaults, grave and obelisk

The Walk

Leave the A671 at the Dog and Partridge and turn east into Church Street. At the end of this are two shippons (barns) with date stones for 1685 and 1691, the latter at the junction with Taylor Street. Turn left into this at the mini-roundabout and walk up past the isolated cottage on the right which was one of the lodgings for the Taylors' patients. Where the road forks with Whitworth Rake going right, head left instead to reach Whitworth House, the Taylors' residence. Pass the Red Lion pub and go up the steps to the churchyard, with the vault, gravestones and obelisk for the Taylor family on the left. Turn left at the edge of the churchyard up rickety steps to the far corner. Here a flagged path marked "Doctors Trail" heads across Doctors' Meadow to the building called Calf Hey, again formerly patients' lodgings. Ignore this path and instead continue up the side of the churchyard to the fine church of St. Bartholomew, built in 1847. Head round the right-hand side of the church and out of the churchyard, turning right to reach a paved lane at a battered "Public Footpath" sign.

Turn right back down the lane, but almost immediately left onto the hillside at a metal "stile" onto a path edged with stone blocks at the right. This leads above Rake Farm on the lane below to a corner by new houses where there is a final view of Whitworth Square. Turn left to a new gateway and continue with pastures to the left and new housing on the right which at first obscures the view of the valley. This however becomes clear around the crossing of a small stream. Just past this, through a wall and fence, turn right on a faint path to descend steeply with a ruined wall on the right. Now the former rail route is visible for the first time in the valley below with bridges over both railway and river. Continue downhill with the stream on the right now in quite a deep valley, to reach a terrace of houses leading down to the A671. Turn left on this for 50 metres and by the Whitworth Arms pub, cross the road to some garages. Head right on a path behind a wall, which descends to the river and a children's playground, before reaching the bridge over the railway seen from the hill above.

Go onto the trackbed and head south in the direction of Rochdale, the route following the pleasant valley of the River Spodden. After about 600 metres, at a clearing on the right shortly before a metal gate, look up to the moor on the right where a clear trackbed can be seen left of an abandoned farm. This was the incline of the Bagden Quarry tramway, used around 1870 to 1900 to bring stone down to Broadley Siding, the site of which is indicated by the stone wall on the right at the end of the clearing. (This siding was also used by a tramway from Spring Mill just to the west.) Behind the siding's stone wall is a complex and puzzling stone structure half-buried in the undergrowth, perhaps to do with the preparation of stone before it was sent away. Continue along the railway, under a ramshackle bridge at the start of Healey Dell Nature Reserve, and along a wooded stretch to reach the single overgrown platform of the former station at Broadley. This had a passing loop, controlled from the signal box which once stood in the obvious gap in the platform. Ignore the station approach road entering at the left and continue down the railway through more woodland to Healey Dell Viaduct (complete with anti-bungee jumping notice!) This gives an airy crossing of the Spodden far below, but its true scale will be seen later.

As the left-hand railings for the viaduct end, turn left through the gate and down stone steps to the road. Turn left on the road to go under the arches, then right at a sign for "Fairy Chapel" to go back beneath them and down towards the river at a weir. At an information board, a stile left allows closer access to the viaduct rearing above, also to the ruins of "Th'Owd Mill i'th' Thrush". These are the scanty remains of a water-powered mill built to "finish" cloth from local handloom weavers. A visit here means retracing steps back to the information board, then continuing down the path to the riverbank. Green railings ahead show the route as it climbs above the river, which can be a foaming torrent along this stretch after wet weather. As the path continues below fern and moss covered crags, a wooden marker "4" points down steps to the "Fairy Chapel", perhaps the most dramatic stretch of scenery on this river. (Again visiting this means retracing steps back to the main path.) Soon after this, steps take the main path out of the gorge to a lane by modern housing. Turn left here to cross a second viaduct over the river, then a bridge over the railway by the site of Broadley station.

Do not descend to the station site, but keep on the track as it swings right to overlook the former platform. Pass a "Nature Reserve" sign and a rough car park on the left, with some scanty remains of Broadley Wood Mill. Swing left onto a cobbled track, passing the mill's small reservoir to climb up to a shelf with extensive views just before Broadley Fold. Turn right to walk along and in front of the buildings, some of them extensively modernised, unlike those at the settlement of Prickshaw visible further up the hill. **(Note – the path may now be diverted away from the buildings at Broadley Fold.)** Head down the slope, following the line of the frontage of Broadley Fold, towards a modern barn. Behind and left of this, the embankment of the Bagden Quarry tramway is particularly clear, including the bridge support at the left as it reached this track. Descend the hill towards the recently demolished Spring Mill and join the reservoir access road as it swings round the mill site, now an eyesore used for fly-tipping. Just at the corner, note the route of the tramway from the mill as it, like the quarry tramway, headed down to Broadley Siding on the railway section walked earlier.

As housing approaches, do not enter the estate, but keep left round the perimeter of the mill site to almost reach a gate in the well-maintained water board wall. Just before the gate, turn right up a clear track, forking right in 120 metres to keep just above the estate. Views along this stretch extend to the church at Whitworth Square, sitting forlornly above modern housing, with the hill of Brown Wardle prominent above. Keep on the path as it becomes paved and then an access road to garages, to pass the drive for "Houses o' th' Hill" on the left. Now watch out for a narrow flagged path entering at a gate on the left, as diagonally across from this a similar flagged path heads right downhill. Take this path right, past the backs of houses, enjoying the last fine views up valley into Rossendale. Cross a road end and turn left at the end of the houses to descend by steps to meet a road at a pond. Turn left on this road, then right into Hall Street, passing entrances to schools, and the United Reformed church. The road crosses the river near a once-fine brick mill, then the course of the railway (now built over with housing) before reaching the A671 diagonally across from the Dog and Partridge.

14. Red Rock route

Adlington

A walk from Red Rock to White Bear sounds more like the Wild West, but this is the West of Greater Manchester, with peaceful strolls along disused railway and canal close to the River Douglas.

Start: Off the B5239, less than two miles east of the A49 at Standish. GR 584099.

Distance: 6.6km (just over 4 miles) on level terrain, though the route can be shortened to 4 or 5km by using canal bridges 65 or 66 (see map). **Note:** as the canal towpath is used by bikes, and the railway (particularly at the southern end) by both bikes and horses, both can be muddy after wet weather.

Map: Almost all the walk is on Explorer 19 "West Pennine Moors" but the start is on Pathfinder 711 "Wigan and Ormskirk". However the route is so straightforward that Landranger 108 (Liverpool) should prove adequate.

By car: The nearest motorway access is from the M6 at junction 27, then east on the A5209 to Standish and the B5239 to Red Rock (see inset map). Access is also possible from M61, junction 6, via Aspull. There is a sizeable car park on the north side of the B5239 at the start of the walk. However, it is not well sign-posted from the road and is easily missed. It is just to the west (towards Standish) of the traffic lights giving one-way access over the canal, with the Crawford Arms pub just further east (towards Aspull)

By public transport: There is a limited bus service (Standish Circular) from Wigan to the Crawford Arms, but access by bus or train would be easier at Adlington (Harrison Road off the A6 leads to the canal at bridge 68).

The Lancashire Union Railway was previously encountered on Walk 5, as jointly responsible with the Lancashire and Yorkshire Railway for building the line from Blackburn to Chorley. Here it was in sole charge of constructing the line from Boar's Head, north of Wigan, to the LYR at Adlington, south of Chorley, which opened in

Arley Hall in its moat makes a picturesque site, viewed from the Leeds and Liverpool Canal *(Gordon Suggitt)*

1869. Both lines were part of a scheme to link East Lancashire to Garston Dock outside Liverpool, via the St Helens Railway (LNWR from 1864). The LYR and LNWR worked the Blackburn-Chorley line, with the latter's trains continuing along the Adlington-Boar's Head section to Wigan. There were two intermediate stations, at Red Rock and White Bear, and two viaducts over the River Douglas. Passenger services at these stations ended as early as 1949, and since the closure of the line to through traffic in 1971, all trace of stations and viaducts has been lost. Only the trackbed between Red Rock and the outskirts of Adlington remains.

The stretch of canal walked is part of the Leeds and Liverpool Canal, but here is known as the "Lancaster Pool". This is the name for the 9-mile level stretch with no locks, which runs from Wigan Locks (see Walk 15) to Wheelton Locks beyond Chorley, and refers to the fact that it was built by the Lancaster Canal Company. It was thus an extension of the "South End" of the Lancaster Canal i.e. the resumption of navigation south of the tramway used on Walk 4. Here it is never further than a quarter of a mile from the River Douglas, which is crossed at the furthest point of the walk.

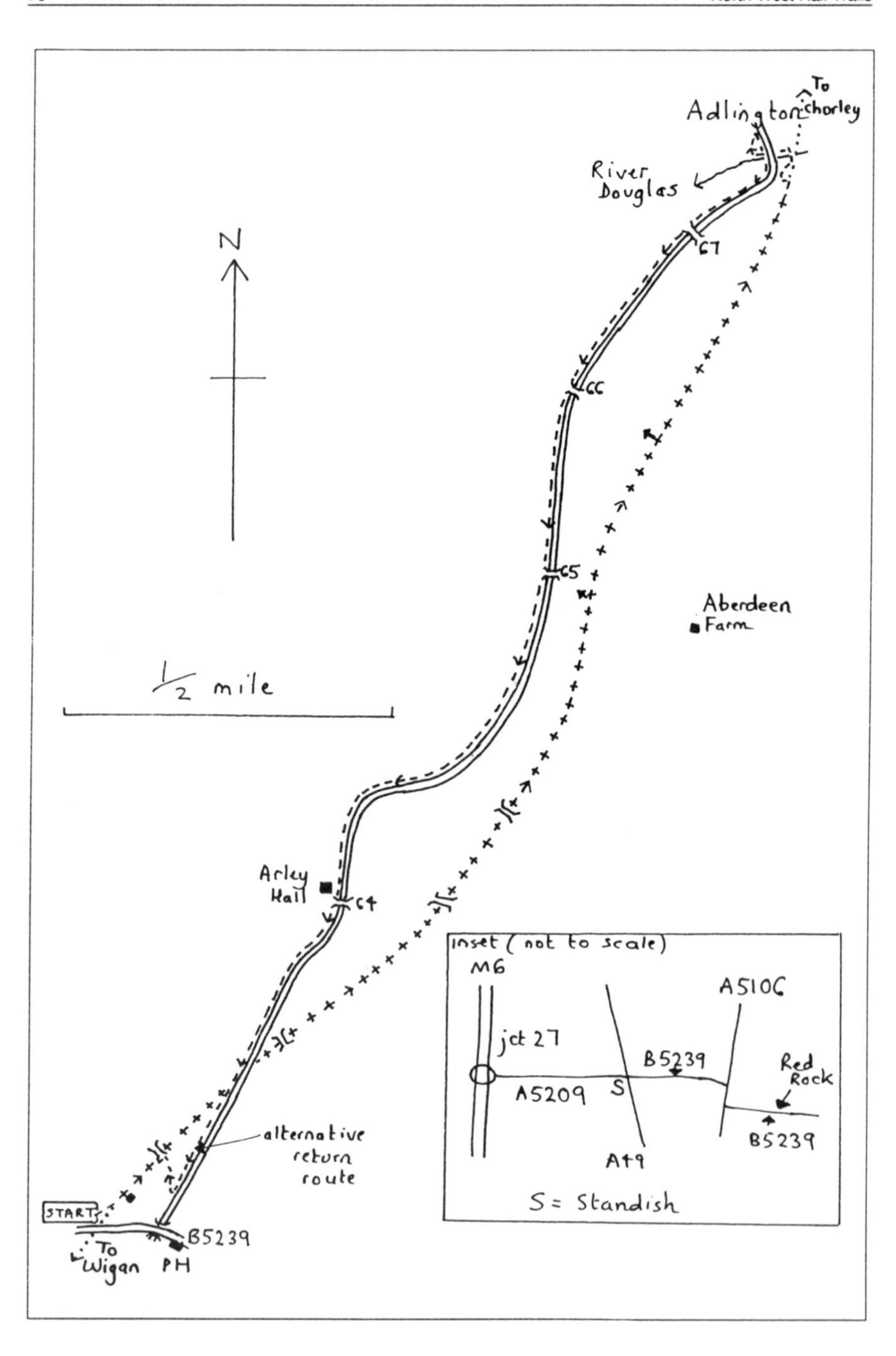
To Chorley
Adlington
River Douglas
N
67
66
65
Aberdeen Farm
1/2 mile
Arley Hall
64
Inset (not to scale)
M6
A5106
jct 27
B5239
Red Rock
A5209
S
B5239
A49
S = Standish
alternative return route
START
To Wigan
B5239
PH

The Walk

Leave the car park at the "horse riders and cyclists" sign. In 120 metres the path bears left at an attractive stone house to join the line of the railway. For the next 1600 metres the line is enclosed in a cutting and is usually quiet and secluded, except at weekends when it can be quite well-used. It is crossed by a succession of bridges, usually stone and brick constructions and mostly for farm access. The canal bridge stands out however, both for its iron construction and for the extreme angle at which it crosses the trackbed. Eventually the cutting eases to allow views to the canal in close proximity to the left and to distant hills on the right. The bridges are replaced by crossing points, usually with double gates across the track. The second of these permits access left to the canal at bridge 65, if a shorter walk is required. Similarly, the next crossing point, marked by a dip where a bridge has been removed, allows access to bridge 66. A concrete cap in the field at the left of this crossing point is a reminder of the coal-mining once found in this now peaceful rural area.

Assuming the full walk is attempted, the line now leads straight towards a distant factory chimney, over an unexpected rise where a bridge over has been filled in, and then suddenly overlooks the canal. Here the path leaves the trackbed and zigzags down left to cross the River Douglas. The railway having taken a sharp bend northwards also crossed the river hereabouts. Now no trace remains of its three-arch viaduct, nor of White Bear station 800 metres further into Adlington. Just over the stream, turn left at a T-junction of paths to pass under the fine stone aqueduct of the canal, then right up steps to gain the canal towpath just short of bridge 68. Turn right on the towpath and follow it back over the aqueduct to a sharp right turn. Keep going on the towpath past bridge 67 with views over the Douglas on the right. There are also views back left to the hills but it is worth waiting for bridge 66 and climbing onto this to admire the panorama. To the right of the view back, Winter Hill's tallest TV mast appears to be built on Rivington Pike with its chunky tower. Further over, the smaller masts rise above the wooded slopes of Lever Park, ending with the Pigeon Tower at the left. Stretching further left still and above the canal are the northern hills of the West Pennine Moors.

Returning to the canal towpath, views are soon lost as like the railway to the left, it is enclosed for most of the journey back to Red Rock. The scenery is pleasant enough, especially once wooded slopes drop away to the right. Eventually bridge 64 approaches, indicated by (mock) castellated buildings to its left. These are part of the outbuildings of Arley Hall, clearly visible on the right just before the bridge. This appears not to be of great antiquity, but makes a charming sight as it sits completely surrounded by a moat. It is now a golf course clubhouse! The canal now almost manages a double bend before a straight stretch leads over the railway. Here a steep descent leads back down to the trackbed, but a safer alternative is to carry on along the towpath towards the road and traffic lights. Just before a landing stage, step down through the hedge at the right, over a missing stile, onto the lane below. Turn right and follow the lane to the railway. Just before the bridge, steps lead down to the trackbed which can be retraced back to the starting point.

15. Hall, railway and canal

Haigh

The estates of Haigh Hall make a pleasant start and finish to this walk whose middle portion includes a dramatic stretch of canal and disused railways – not surprising considering the proximity of Wigan.

Start: The main car park at Haigh Hall, two and a half miles north-east of Wigan. GR 597088.

Distance: 8km (5 miles) with 77 metres (250 ft) of height gain, though slopes are mostly gentle.

Map: Pathfinders 711 "Wigan and Ormskirk" and 712 "Bolton (South)".

By car: Follow the signs for Haigh Hall from the B5238 at New Springs, or the B5239 at Haigh and between Haigh and Red Rock/Standish. Note that there is a charge for parking at Haigh Hall.

By public transport: A start at Haigh Hall would not be possible, but the circuit can be walked from the two points at which it intersects with the B5238 Wigan-Aspull road, which has frequent bus services to Blackrod, Bolton etc. These give access to the "Whelley Loop" disused railway close to the Alexandra pub, and the canal at bridge 59A (alight at the Crown Hotel where access to the towpath is just to the right of the road bridge).

Many of the features of interest seen on this walk owe their origin to the former owners of Haigh Hall, the Earls of Crawford and Balcarres. Only the Great Sough dates back to their predecessors – the Bradshaighs who owned the estate for almost five centuries to 1780. This was a mine tunnel constructed for Sir Roger Bradshaigh in 1652 to drain his coal workings. By 1780, the estate had passed by marriage to Alexander Lindsay, 23rd Earl of Crawford and Balcarres who probably had the greatest impact on the area, though not on its railways. However his Haigh Foundry, set up as an ironworks with his brother Robert in 1788, produced over 100 locomotives between

1812 and 1856, starting with the first built in Lancashire – "The Walking Horse"!

In addition, Alexander rebuilt the pre-Tudor mansion of the Bradshaighs between 1830 and 1844 to produce Haigh Hall as it is today, and was a investor in the Lancaster Canal's southern extension across his estates, opened in 1798. This was originally meant to extend to Westhoughton, but in 1816 was incorporated into the Leeds and Liverpool Canal, which built its route up 21 locks at Wigan to meet and use the Lancaster Canal past Chorley (see Walk 14). He also developed the area's collieries, whose rail links within this area were built for his successor, the 24th Earl. The first of these was a line from pits near Aspull, across the canal at bridge 59B, and across the southern edges of the estate to Haigh Foundry. It only lasted from 1856 to 1869, until the construction of the Lancashire Union Railway line across the estate. This included a branch serving the foundry from the north instead, and was part of a scheme to link East Lancashire with St Helens and Garston Dock, then outside Liverpool.

The Haigh Hall section of this line was opened between Haigh Junction and Ince Moss Junction in 1869, initially for goods, but three years later saw one of the shortest-lived passenger services ever. From January to March 1872, trains ran from a station at Whelley to Liverpool! The station then closed, never to re-open, and the line reverted to freight only. However, in the 1880s, the LNWR built connections from the LUR line to the main line both north and south of Wigan. This meant that the section past Haigh Hall now became part of the "Whelley Loop", much used by freight trains by-passing Wigan. Connections with both the LNWR and Lancashire and Yorkshire Railway lines from Manchester to Wigan allowed use of the loop by such passenger services as Manchester to Blackpool (via Tyldesley) and Manchester to Windermere. The 1960s saw heavy use of the loop while the main line was electrified through Wigan, but once this was completed the loop went out of use in 1974.

Now the rail route is walkable from Haigh Hall to Hindley – part of the switch from industrial to leisure activities which is particularly marked in this area where Haigh Hall itself passed to Wigan

Borough in 1947 and is now used for functions. Its estate is now a country park, and the canal is now used for cruising; its industrial use has gone with the works that once lined its banks, though the Haigh Foundry site continues in industrial use.

The former Whelley station house was still standing in 1964, despite its use for railway purposes lasting only a few months in 1872! *(J. Peden collection)*

The Walk

Leave the car park in the direction of the hall, and walk past the stable block. This was refurbished in 1989 and now includes an information centre, gift shop, cafe, and craft gallery. Continue down to the hall and round the building to its impressive frontage. The tarmac drive leading south-east from here can now be followed for some two and a half kilometres through the estate, crossing bridges over first the canal and then the disused railway. However the estate is said to have 60km of paths, made to provide employment during the cotton famine of the 1860s, and it is worth using some of these to provide variety on the route. The first of these leads right about 170 metres after the miniature railway has swung away left. After passing through woodland on the approximate site of the workings

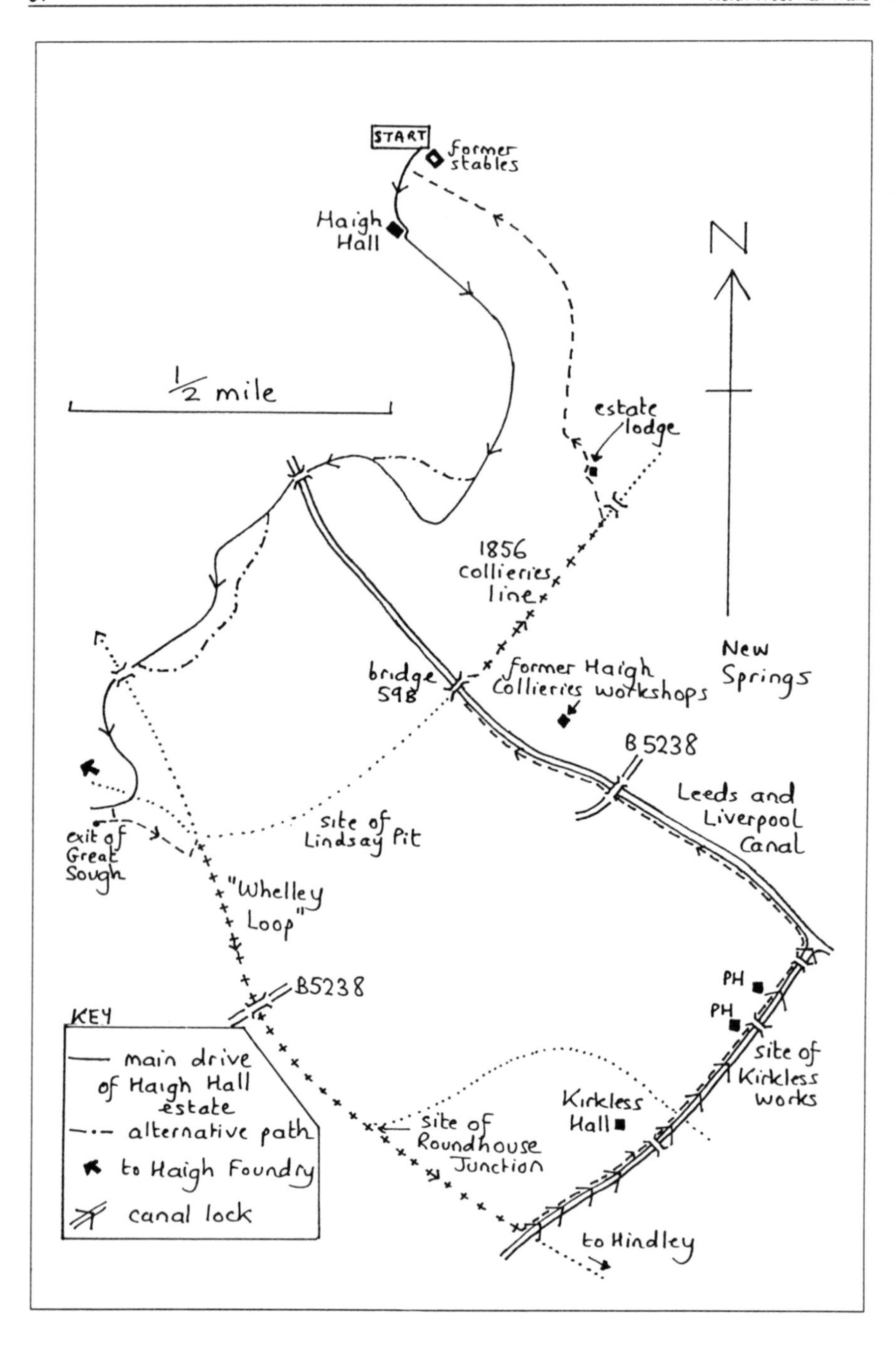

START
former stables
Haigh Hall
N
½ mile
estate lodge
1856 collieries line
bridge 59B
former Haigh Collieries workshops
New Springs
B5238
Leeds and Liverpool Canal
exit of Great Sough
site of Lindsay Pit
"Whelley Loop"
B5238
PH
PH
site of Kirkless works
Kirkless Hall
site of Roundhouse Junction
to Hindley
KEY
main drive of Haigh Hall estate
alternative path
to Haigh Foundry
canal lock

drained by the Great Sough, the path rejoins the tarmac shortly before the canal bridge. The second path roughly parallels the tarmac drive to its left between the two bridges.

The second bridge gives the first view of the former "Whelley Loop" line, which is far from encouraging. The line was originally sunk here below a cut-and-cover tunnel to preserve the scenery of the estate. This and later subsidence have left a cutting which is often flooded and choked with vegetation. Thus it is best to stay with the tarmac drive which at least allows a visit to the Great Sough.

About 300 metres after the bridge, the drive swings in a huge bend right and there is a stone marker with a boot print sign where a broad track heads off left. Hereabouts was the crossing point of the 1856 railway to Haigh Foundry. Keep on the drive for another 30 metres until rough stone steps lead down left. These are rather overgrown and easily missed. At the foot of the steps, turn right alongside the stream, which is reasonably clear. However after 40 metres, the water suddenly becomes bright orange-yellow in colour. This marks the exit of the Great Sough, which cannot itself be seen from this bank. For a clearer view, continue for another 40 metres to a footbridge. Cross this and walk back on the far bank to overlook the exit which is a metre-wide brick arch still discharging over 2 million litres of water daily from underground workings. Retrace the route back to the foot of the overgrown steps and carry on with the stream on the right. The path soon crosses the broad track seen earlier and heads up and round to the left to reach the remains of a concrete footbridge (again roughly on the route of the 1856 line). Just to the right, the trackbed of the "Whelley Loop" is now accessible and walkable.

Turn right along the trackbed. To the left, areas landscaped with young trees mark the site of Lindsay Pits before the track reaches the Whelley Road bridge, where it is rather rubbish-strewn. Just past the bridge, there is a slope down to the railway from the left (to the site of Whelley Station?), followed by the former Roundhouse junction where a branch led off left towards Kirkless works. Keep straight on however to reach the canal just down from lock 73.

The trackbed continues on the far side and is walkable as far as Hindley, 2km away, but the route for this walk turns left on the canal towpath to pass the top nine locks of the 21 in the Wigan flight. It is worth a glance at one of these to study their massive stonework, which includes 1816 date stones and lock number stones (in Roman numerals, working down from the top lock which is 1). To the right of the canal is the site of the Kirkless Iron and Steelworks, operational from the 1860s to closure in 1930. Not much remains of this once extensive works, just slag heaps overlooking lock 73, the bridge abutments where the railway from Roundhouse Junction crossed the canal (up from lock 68) and a retaining brick wall soon after. To the left, by lock 69, is the striking farmhouse of Kirkless Hall, then the two pubs either side of lock 66 and the lock-keeper's house at the top lock (65).

Above the top lock, the canal forms a T-junction where the Leeds and Liverpool was built to meet the Lancaster which continues SE for 250 metres on its projected course to Westhoughton. Turn left to follow the canal back towards Haigh Hall, with an isolated remnant of the Albion Iron Works across from the junction. Continue along the towpath towards bridge 59A where the Wigan-Aspull road (B5238) crosses. Pass under the bridge and follow the canal as it bends right, with a building like a small hall with a green-topped bell tower over on the right. This is all that remains of the central workshops of the Haigh and Aspull collieries once owned by the Earls of Crawford and Balcarres. At bridge 59B, take the path up to the left and cross the bridge. This marks the route of the 1856 line to Haigh Foundry (its route down to the SW corner of the estate can be seen over to the left).

The route of the railway can be followed up and slightly to the right of the bridge, leading through woodland to metal gates after about 400 metres. Past these, the track is on an embankment with a stream below on the left. Soon after, a bridge appears ahead, with more gates below it. Leave the track about 35 metres before the bridge and head through the woods on the left towards the red-roofed lodge building marking the entrance back into the Haigh Hall estate. Go left round the back of the lodge, and along to the miniature railway track. Cross this and turn sharp right, past another "bootprint" marker and a large pond on the right to re-cross the rail track at the hut which serves as an engine shed. Continue generally straight on until the Hall garden wall appears ahead, then bear left past the stone lion and "crazy golf"/ model village, through the children's playground to the stables with the car park beyond.

16. Around the Flash

Pennington

Short sections of disused railway and part of the Leeds and Liverpool Canal are used on this circuit of Pennington Flash, a country park formed from areas left derelict by coal-mining.

Start: The main car park at Pennington Flash Country Park, SW of Leigh. GR 644990.

Distance: 7.2km (nearly 4½ miles) on almost level terrain, with mostly well-maintained paths.

Map: Pathfinder 723 "Eccles (Greater Manchester)".

By car: The main entrance for the country park is on the A572 Leigh to Newton-le-Willows road, 2 miles SW of Leigh. It can be easily reached from the M6 at junction 23 via the East Lancs Road (A580). Once in the park, follow the drive round to the main car park which is now sited to the NE of the lake (see map). There is a small charge for parking.

By public transport: The main entrance on the A572 is passed by buses between Leigh and Wigan/ Warrington, also Leigh-Lowton local services. The access drive for cars can be avoided by using a parallel path, slightly closer to the lake, as far as the bridge over the Pennington Brook. On the return journey, after Sorrowcow Farm, avoid left turns to keep close to the park perimeter to reach the main entrance.

Pennington Flash is a 70-hectare lake which formed in the thirteen years to 1905 as coal-mining in the area both lowered the land and blocked natural drainage. The areas around it became wasteland as collieries and railways closed, and were not improved by the tipping of vast quantities of waste, both from coal-mining and household refuse. Despite this, the lake developed as a centre for fishing and sailing, and its recreational potential began to be fully used from 1981, when the area was opened as a country park.

The first railway in the area was the Bolton and Leigh (1828) as described in Walk 18, but this is now the A579 past Leigh. First among those walked on this route was the 12 mile Glazebrook to Wigan (Central) line of 1879. This was built by the Wigan Junction Railway for coal traffic but operated from the start by the Manchester, Sheffield and Lincolnshire Railway (Great Central from 1897). Passenger services came in 1884, with trains from Wigan to Manchester Central, and, with the addition of a curve at Glazebrook, Wigan to Warrington from 1900. The only intermediate stations within the scope of this walk were at West Leigh and Bradford, and Lowton St Mary's. An 8 mile branch was also built to serve St Helens, which provided passenger services only from 1900 to 1952. Goods provision lasted a little longer, from 1895 to 1965. Around the later date, all services north of Lowton St Mary's ended.

Between these two (eventual) Great Central incursions came the Pennington to Platt Bridge line of 1885, built by the LNWR to serve this area of the Lancashire Coalfield. For this purpose, a branch was built at the same time north to the canal where it linked with lines serving the Westleigh collieries. These mines had all closed by 1937, and the branch was lifted six years later. In addition, a complex "flyover", built in 1903 east of the lake, allowed the "main" line to also be used by passenger trains between Leigh and Wigan, for which an intermediate station was built at Plank Lane. This only lasted until 1915, and passenger services ended completely in 1942. Freight services lasted until 1963, but coal trains continued to use the line north of the canal up to the closure of Bickershaw Colliery in 1992.

Very little remains elsewhere of any of these lines, although a stretch of the first Great Central line has been made into a linear park at Culcheth (access at GR 649949). Much more lasting has been the impact of the Leeds and Liverpool Canal, in the form of its branch from Wigan to meet the Bridgewater Canal at Leigh, opened in 1820. This was originally built with four locks, two of which became unnecessary as the land around the canal sank due to the mining subsidence that created the Flash. Even today, the canal is high on an embankment built from pit waste.

The garden is apparently the subject of this 1912 study of Pennington station on the Bolton and Leigh Line, now used as the A579 past Leigh! *(J. Ryan collection)*

The Walk

Continue from the car park along the lake shore. The unsurfaced path closer to the water's edge corresponds roughly to the LNWR lines of 1885/1903. On the right is the building which serves as an information point with toilets, and just past this a children's playground. Beyond this the main LNWR lines disappear into bushes leading to the lake, but the route swings right as a broad path which soon follows the branch line built to meet colliery lines at the canal. At first this goes through quite dense woodland but this thins out, and there are views over lake inlets and lagoons to both left and right by the hide which is well-placed for observing the area's teeming birdlife. Continue on the path as it bends sharp left (away from the LNWR branch) and approaches the canal embankment.

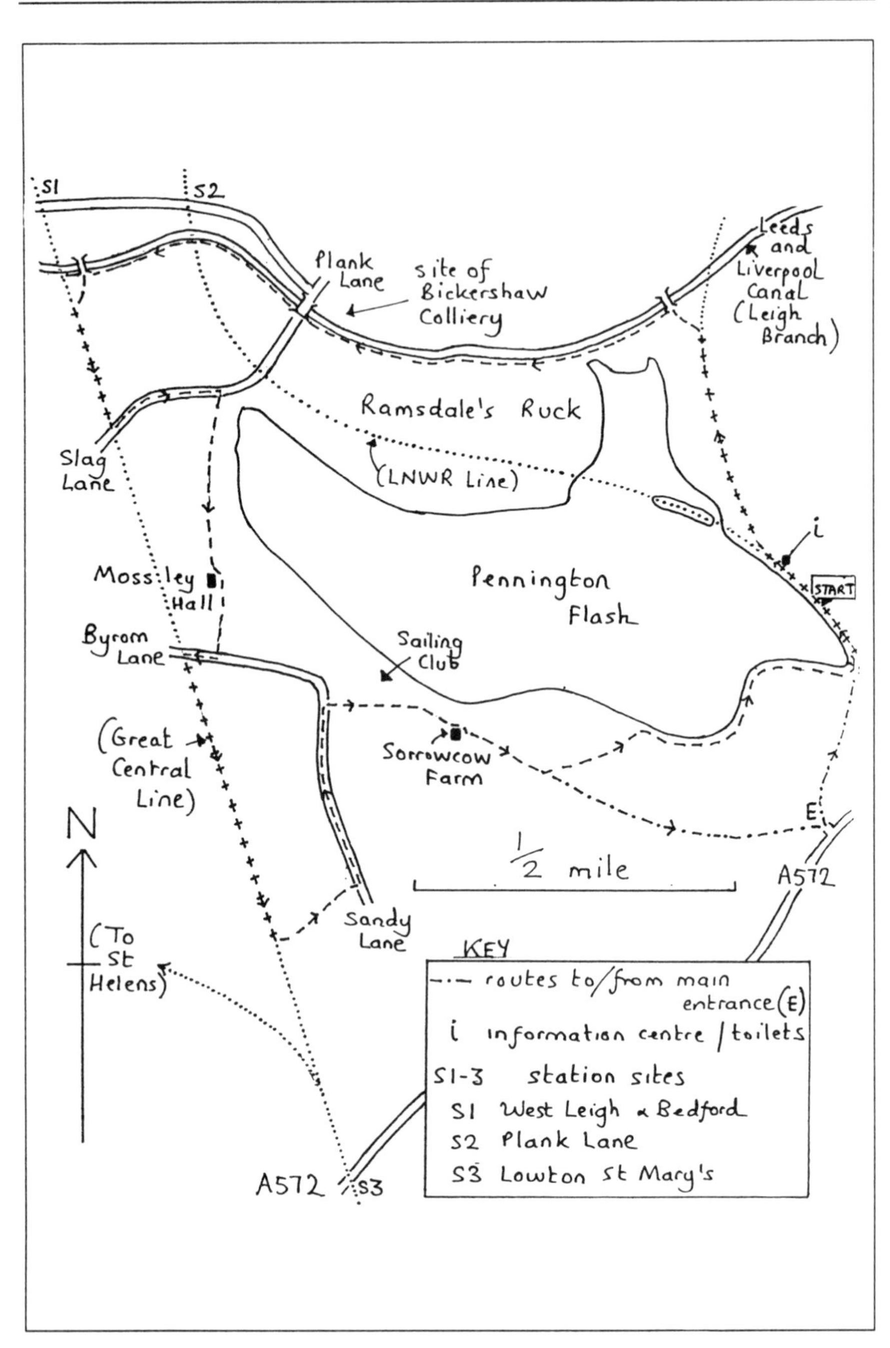
S1
S2
Plank Lane
site of Bickershaw Colliery
Leeds and Liverpool Canal (Leigh Branch)
Ramsdale's Ruck
(LNWR Line)
Slag Lane
Moss ley Hall
Pennington Flash
i
START
Byrom Lane
Sailing Club
Sorrowcow Farm
(Great Central Line)
E
N
1/2 mile
A572
Sandy Lane
(To St Helens)
KEY
routes to/from main entrance (E)
i information centre / toilets
S1-3 station sites
S1 West Leigh & Bedford
S2 Plank Lane
S3 Lowton St Mary's
A572
S3

Go up the concrete steps to reach the canal at a footbridge. Turn left on the towpath and as the canal swings right there are good views over the northern inlet of the Flash, including the "spit" of land at its entrance which indicates the route of the LNWR "main" line. The canal now bends left then right, with the massive spoil heap known as Ramsdale's Ruck on the left. It is estimated that 6 million cubic metres of colliery waste were dumped here, completely obliterating the LNWR line as it left the Flash. Over to the right of the canal was Bickershaw Colliery, whose mine headgear dominated the landscape here until recently. Now almost no trace remains, with only a hint of formerly extensive loading staithes along the canal. Next is Plank Lane, which crosses the canal by a lift bridge just by the once-imposing Britannia Hotel of 1903. Cross the road, keeping the bridge to the right, and continue on the towpath as the canal bends left. Here the bridgeworks of the LNWR line can clearly be seen, though this would hardly give sufficient clearance today due to the raising of the canal. The short-lived Plank Lane station (1903-1915) was just to the north though nothing is left at the site. Follow the canal towpath towards a bridge, just past which are the more substantial bridgeworks of the Great Central line. This is on the north side only as the embankment has been removed in the first field to the south, necessitating a return to the bridge.

Take the path up to the right to reach the farm track at the bridge. By crossing the bridge, it is possible to reach the site of West Leigh and Bedford station, but here too almost nothing remains so it is better to turn right along the farm track, away from the canal and towards the railway. Within 100 metres, as the track bends right, there is access left up onto the embankment which can then be followed to a missing bridge over a road. Although the embankment is visible across the road, a stream is in the way preventing access. It is best to turn left along the road, past Slag Lane Waste Disposal Site until the road begins to bend left, where a path without a signpost leads right over a concrete footbridge and a stile. Just past these there are views left over the Flash and right to the embankment.

The path becomes a track leading towards a farm (Mossley Hall) where stiles take the path left to by-pass the buildings before the farm access lane is reached. Follow this to a gate where it meets a road (Byrom Lane). Turn right here and within 100 metres, just over the railway bridge, steps lead down to the trackbed, which here is very overgrown although there is a clear path, often along the left-hand side. Follow along the railway for about 800 metres, watching out for routes crossing the line. The first of these is a farm track and then there are two paths. The second of these marks the end of the rail route on this walk. It is possible to continue along the railway to the A572 at Lowton St Mary's, where the station site has been built over. This would include the junction with the St Helens branch, which is still walkable for a short distance but soon becomes overgrown. Thus it is better to view the branch before leaving the railway at the second path crossing, where it can be seen as a curved line of trees across the field on the right.

Turn left to face a gate and a stile. Go over the stile and keep to the left edge of the field to reach a further stile at its top corner. Cross this to reach a road (Sandy Lane). Although there appear to be paths between here and Sorrowcow Farm, these are very overgrown; it is best to turn left on the road and follow it past Red House Farm on the left and the entrance to Rowe Farm on the right, to reach a right turn into the sailing club access lane (Green Lane). Turn into this and pass the sailing HQ on the left. As the lane bends right, there is a good view of the full expanse of the Flash with Ramsdale's Ruck dominating the far shore. Head through the yard of Sorrowcow Farm, keeping the bungalow over to the right, to signs showing the path heading right. Keep on this clear path through gateways and over a bridge to a T-junction of paths. The main entrance can be reached by keeping straight on here, but to return to the main car park, turn left here then left again at a picnic table and right along the lake shore. This leads round the eastern end of the lake back to the car park, but note the footbridge crossing the Pennington Brook which is built on the bridgeworks of the original LNWR line (its route is roughly followed by the path from the footbridge back alongside the car park).

17. Where coal was king

Tyldesley

Although coal-mining has gone completely from the small town of Tyldesley, it is still almost ringed by the disused railways from that era which are used in this circuit.

Start: Tyldesley Square in the centre of the town. GR 691020.

Distance: 6.3km (almost 4 miles) with only 33 metres (100 ft) height variation.

Map: Pathfinder 712 "Bolton (South)".

By car: Tyldesley is on the A577 between Wigan and junction 13 on the M60 at Worsley, and has plenty of central car parking. However, access is rather complicated by the A-road following a one-way system through the town centre. This is shown on the inset map, with parking areas marked 'P'. Blossom Street is closer to the Square, but gets busy especially on market day (Friday). There is usually space off Primrose Street, only two blocks away, if required.

By public transport: Tyldesley is well-served by buses from Wigan, Bolton and Manchester, though the one-way system means separate town centre locations for the bus stops – see inset map.

Although most disused railways in the area were for collieries, the first one on this walk was the LNWR line from Eccles (Manchester) to Wigan, opened in 1864. The section east from Ellenbrook is dealt with in Walk 20. This western part had stations at Ellenbrook, Tyldesley, Howe Bridge (just before a connection with the Bolton and Leigh Railway), Hindley Green and Platt Bridge before Wigan (North Western). Just west of Tyldesley, the line split with a branch heading SW through Leigh to the Bolton and Leigh at Pennington Junction. Later connections via Great Central tracks to the "Whelley Loop" (see Walk 15) allowed use of the line through Tyldesley by expresses from Manchester to Blackpool, Windermere and Keswick, as well as local services. These declined from the 1950s with Howe

A railtour visits Tyldesley station in 1966, two years before the end of normal passenger services on this line. *(Author's collection)*

Bridge station closing in 1959, followed by Ellenbrook, Hindley Green and Platt Bridge two years later. Tyldesley kept its passenger services until 1968, but the whole line (including the Leigh branch) closed the following year, apart from colliery traffic, which continued for some years. Most of this line, including the Leigh branch, is still walkable, from the A577 at Parr Brow (GR 713018), through Tyldesley to Leigh and Howe Bridge.

Two colliery branches are also walked here, first the Chanters branch built to the LNWR a mile west of Tyldesley station in the 1860s. Chanters, actually in Atherton, was one of the major pits of this area of the Lancashire Coalfield and was regularly upgraded from the 1890s through to the 1920s. At its closure in 1964-6, it was the last remaining pit of the once numerous Atherton Collieries group. A second colliery railway system was built east of Tyldesley. It too started in the 1860s and joined Combermere and Peelwood collieries to both the LNWR and the Bridgewater Canal. Peelwood also had access to the Lancashire and Yorkshire Railway east of Central Station (Atherton). Combermere closed in 1893, but its site was occupied by a brickworks which used the line between the two collieries for access to the LYR. However by 1939 both Peelwood and the brickworks had closed and the branch was disused.

The Walk

Cross the road from the square and walk down Astley Street, with Tyldesley Chapel (1719) on the right. Within 200 metres, Public Footpath signs point right to "Leigh and Howe Bridge". This is the start of the former LNWR part of the walk. Turning right brings the route onto the site of Tyldesley station, nothing of which remains, as the whole area has been landscaped with trees on the station site and a grassy field where extensive sidings once were to the left. Proceeding along the approximate line of the trackbed, in about 400 metres a fenced-off area of trees marks the site of St George's Colliery, where once rail lines headed off left to the strangely named Gin Pit and Nook Pits. Soon after this the path splits. The less well-used path off to the left follows the line of the branch to Leigh, which can be seen crossing the fields ahead. Keep on the more used path to the right, which soon reaches another signpost. Again take the right fork, this time sign-posted "Howe Bridge". This is a narrow path through lots of undergrowth, but after crossing a road it becomes a broader straight track leading past a school on the right. Cross a small stream by a wooden bridge as the path narrows again. As power lines approach, there is quite a sharp dip to a farm lane. This marks the end of the LNWR line as far this walk is concerned.

Turn right along the lane and up a slight rise, under the power lines, there is a junction of paths. Take the second on the right, sign-posted "Hindsford". This is the former Chanters branch which soon crosses a gully, particularly deep to the left, and becomes a broad grassy swathe heading back towards Tyldesley. Housing appears, first to the right, then on the left below a church with a tower.

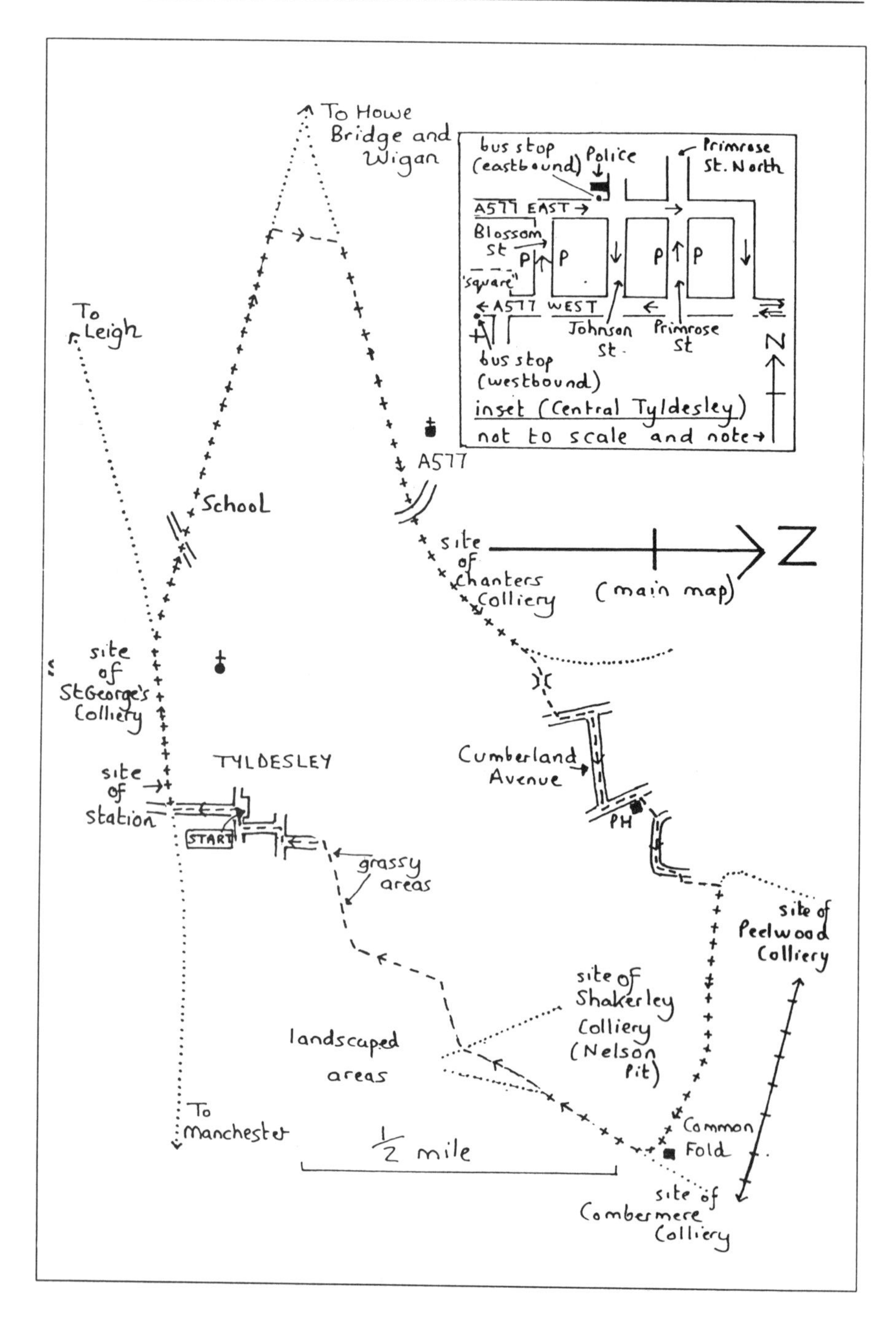
To Howe Bridge and Wigan
bus stop (eastbound)
Police
Primrose St. North
A577 EAST
Blossom St
'square'
P
A577 WEST
Johnson St
Primrose St
bus stop (westbound)
N
inset (Central Tyldesley) not to scale and note
To Leigh
School
A577
site of Chanters Colliery
(main map)
site of St George's Colliery
TYLDESLEY
Cumberland Avenue
site of station
START
PH
grassy areas
site of Peelwood Colliery
site of Shakerley Colliery (Nelson Pit)
landscaped areas
To Manchester
1/2 mile
Common Fold
site of Combermere Colliery

Two concrete covers to the left of the track seem to be over drainage from underground workings. Just along from these, the track reaches the A577. Cross the busy road diagonally left, then bear right to pick up the line of the Chanters branch again. Continue on the colliery line with new housing to the right. Heading left into the next straight stretch, the fenced-off area of trees on the left marks the site of Chanters Colliery. The path now often splits here, not surprisingly as the colliery line itself comprised seven tracks in this area! For the moment keep left following the fence line, as a small valley becomes visible on the right. However as housing appears above the valley ahead, leave the route of the colliery line by forking right down to a footbridge over the stream and carry on up the slope to the housing estate.

Turn left along the road through the housing estate, then first right into Cumberland Avenue. At the end of this, turn left to walk past the Homeground pub on the right. Just past the pub, turn right after a fence to take a tarmac path through to a road of bungalows and semi-detached houses. Turn right on this and follow the road round left to an empty patch on the right, with "No Tipping" notices. Go across this patch on a clear path which turns left at a field with views ahead of massive spoil heaps, surprisingly still not landscaped. Go along this path with the backs of houses to the left till it meets a track at a T-junction. Turn right on this track which follows the route of the former branch linking Peelwood and Combermere Collieries. There are now open views on both sides. To the right past fields (where once was Shakerley Colliery's Nelson Pit) is Tyldesley on a slight ridge, its church standing out well. On the left a yellow and brown bridge marks the route of the only rail line still open in the area – the Lancashire and Yorkshire line from Manchester to Wigan, opened in 1888.

Follow the track as it bends right past Common Fold farm buildings, and at a gate turn right into a broad lane leading back towards Tyldesley. This was the route of the line from Combermere Colliery, although it was actually on the grassy stretch at the left, railway and lane sharing this route for the next 300 metres. At a track entering from the left however, the railway headed slightly left to eventually reach the LNWR east of Tyldesley. Its course is soon lost in the landscaped hills formed from the spoil heaps of Cleworth Hall Colliery. Over on the right, a clear embankment marks the course of an earlier line from Shakerley Colliery (Nelson Pit) which too disappears into the landscaping. Continue along the lane as it bends right, over the Shakerley Colliery railway, and along to a bungalow and farm on the right. Pass these and turn left, over a stream, to reach a grassy area in front of the outlying terraces of Tyldesley. Turn right to cross the grassy area, and as it first narrows and then widens to a second open area, take the first street off on the left. This is Primrose Street North, which leads back to the car park or bus stop as required – see inset map.

18. In the beginning

The Chequerbent Incline

Despite its obscurity, this forerunner of NW rail routes offers plenty of evidence of its origins and later changes, though little remains from its coal-mining past.

Start: Chequerbent roundabout, where the A6 meets the A58, 2 miles SW of Bolton. GR 671062.

Distance: 4.8km (3 miles), with about 55 metres (175 feet) of ascent.
Note: This walk, especially parts of the incline itself, can be very muddy indeed—definitely a case of walking boots or wellies. (This does not apply to the features close to the A6 at Chequerbent shown on the inset map).

Map: Pathfinder 712 "Bolton South".

By car: The present A6 west of the roundabout has been realigned leaving a disused stretch by Chequerbent post office available for parking.

By public transport: Chequerbent is well served by bus services, especially from Bolton and Wigan.

Despite the fame of the Liverpool and Manchester Railway, it cannot claim to be the oldest public railway in NW England. It was preceded by two years by the opening in 1828 of the Bolton and Leigh Railway. Built to link Bolton's cotton mills with the Leeds and Liverpool Canal at Leigh, seven miles away, it was engineered by George Stephenson. Its original route involved relatively level stretches with two inclines, at Daubhill and Chequerbent, worked by stationary engines. Early power on the level included some famous locomotives such as Robert Stephenson's "Lancashire Witch", which was used for the opening ceremony. Among early innovations were excursions by rail, including a trip to Newton Races from Bolton as early as 1831. Regular passenger services began the same year, and seven years later over 86,000 passengers were being carried annually. The LNWR took over in 1846 and for 40 years ran the line as a minor branch. However in 1885 the line was made double-track, with deviations to ease the gradient on the two inclines, where cable operation had ended some thirty years earlier. The original Bolton and Leigh line at Chequerbent remained in use for colliery traffic until 1934. The LNWR deviations included new stations at Daubhill and Chequerbent, but local services declined after 1945 leading to those two stations closing in 1952, followed by the loss of passenger services altogether two years later. Holiday trains from Bolton to North Wales continued to use the line for another five years, and it closed finally with the end of colliery traffic in 1969. Much of its route is still identifiable outside central Bolton, but over three miles of line through Leigh are now the A579.

The Chequerbent incline dropped roughly 200ft (61 metres) in 1¼ miles from the high ground SW of Bolton to Atherton, with the Bolton and Leigh version worked by a stationary 50 horse-power engine housed south of the present A6. Its track was laid on over 33,000 stone blocks, some of which are still in position. Even the LNWR deviation of the incline route resulted in gradients originally of 1 in 30, which were increased to as much as 1 in 18.5 by mining subsidence. This was one of the steepest gradients anywhere on British passenger lines.

The area of the incline was developed for coal-mining by Hulton Collieries in the late 19th century. Originally, there was only a small pit just south of the Bolton and Leigh level crossing. By 1870 this had been replaced by Chequerbent Pits 1 and 2, but the main expansion came at the turn of the century, with Bank Pits 1 and 2 (further down the incline) sunk in the 1890s, and Bank Pits 3 and 4 over half a mile to the east in 1900. These last two pits, known locally as Pretoria Pit, were served by an extension eastwards from the railway, and were the scene of the Lancashire coalfield's worst accident when in 1910 an explosion killed 344 men and boys. Despite this tragedy, all the mines continued in operation until after the First World War, with Bank Pits 3 and 4 the last to close in 1934. Now extensive landscaping has been done and there is little evidence that mining ever took place here.

A train out of Bolton Moor Street at Atherton Bag Lane in 1954, the year passenger services ended. Now, only the distinctively gabled Railway Hotel remains from this scene. *(Author's collection)*

The Walk

The starting point is close to the attractively restored Rose Cottage. This was built as a handloom weaver's cottage, and is one of the few old buildings left at Chequerbent since the construction of the huge A6 roundabout. Walk past the Post Office and cross Park Road (A58 to St Helens) to the end of Ravenswood Terrace (1907). Note how this complements Maypole Terrace (1905) with the Post Office at its end. These dates are indicative of the late-industrial age of most remaining buildings at Chequerbent. Continue across the south side of the roundabout, and along the A6 eastwards for 100 metres. At the end of the brick terraces on the left (Hilton's Terrace – 1889), take the stone-setted track left, sign-posted "Public Footpath". As this heads

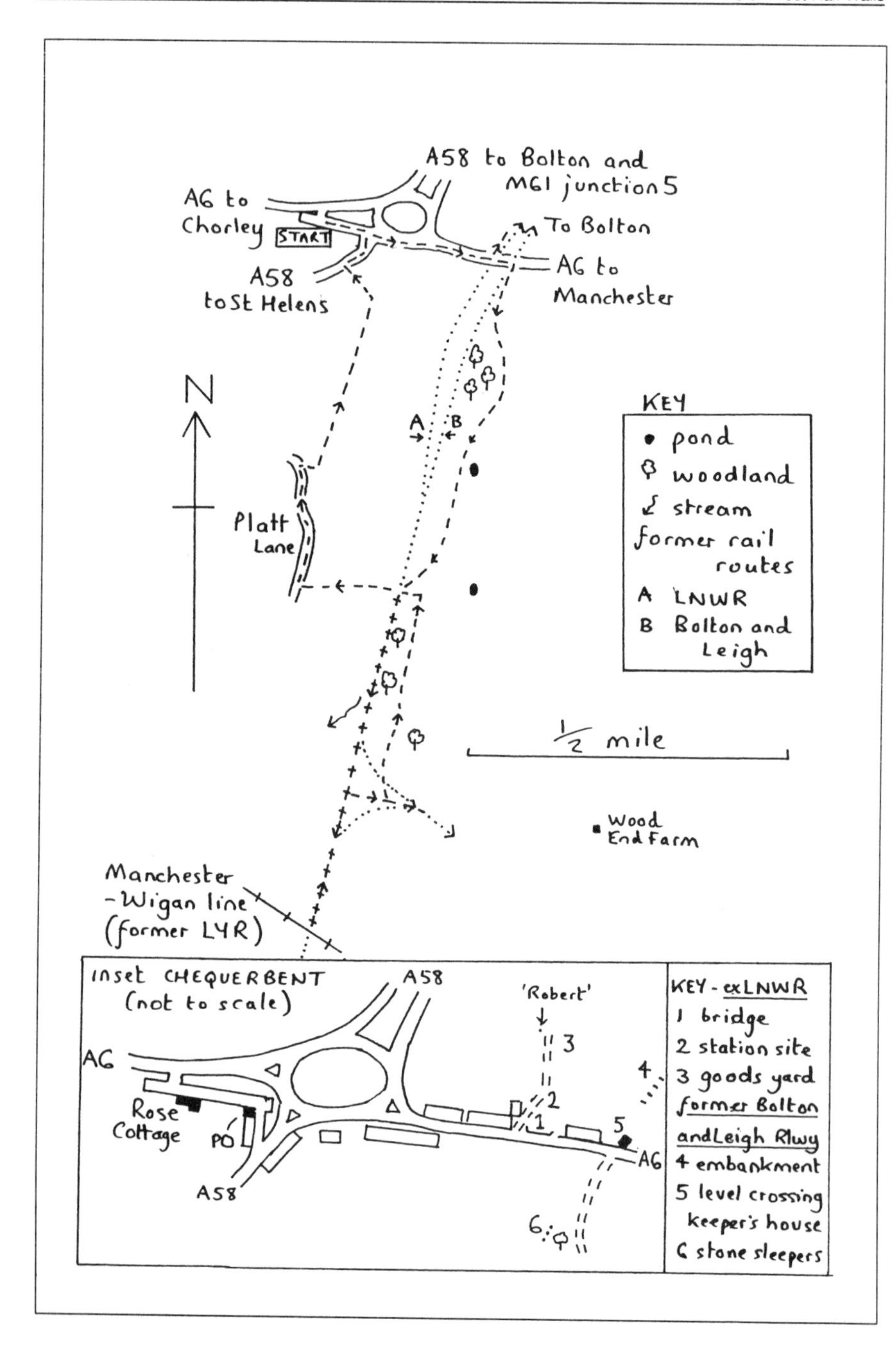
A58 to Bolton and M61 junction 5
A6 to Chorley
START
To Bolton
A6 to Manchester
A58 to St Helens
N
A
B
KEY
pond
woodland
stream
former rail routes
A LNWR
B Bolton and Leigh
Platt Lane
1/2 mile
Wood End Farm
Manchester - Wigan line (former LYR)
inset CHEQUERBENT (not to scale)
A58
'Robert'
A6
Rose Cottage
PO
A58
A6
KEY - ex LNWR
1 bridge
2 station site
3 goods yard
former Bolton and Leigh Rlwy
4 embankment
5 level crossing keeper's house
6 stone sleepers

down towards the M61, the site of the LNWR station is on the right, with the goods yard and sidings straight ahead. At the corner, the view through the fence shows the embankment of the original 1828 line clearly visible over to the right. Continue down the track to the premises of Jose K. Gordon Holt Ltd where just inside the yard are the rusting remains of "Robert". This saddle tank 0-6-0 loco was built at Bristol in 1912, spent most of its working life at Garswood Hall Collieries near Wigan, and is a last survivor of many such locos that came here to be broken up in the 1960s.

Return to the A6, noting the fine "Over Hulton" milestone opposite. Turn left and continue 120 metres along the road, passing the stone bridgework on the left over the former LNWR line. The pebble-dashed cottage set diagonally to the road ("Hope Cottage" 1828) incorporates the former Bolton and Leigh line crossing-keeper's house, and has a small blue plaque commemorating the railway. Cross the A6 to the track heading south, with two "Public Footpath" signs. Go along this track, with modern buildings on the right. Past these, over to the right in the trees, is the route of the LNWR line. Continue on the track towards a small wood, bearing left away from the 1828 line. This can be seen as a low embankment heading past the right of the wood, still with several original stone sleepers in place. Some have two holes visible, where the chairs for the rails were fastened. Back on the track, go past the wood (planted on the site of Chequerbent Pits 1 and 2) and through two gates, which may be open. The track now swings right and left to end at a gate and stile by a small pond used for angling, but carry straight on along the field with a ditch and fence to the left, heading for a "bump" on the skyline. Nearing a second pond on the left, bear right to a battered white sign by a gate and stile.

Cross the stile to a path running right to left. This follows the combined Bolton and Leigh / LNWR lines, which came together about 100 metres further up the slope and used the 1828 route from here down through Atherton. Turn left and follow the path down. This next 200 metres can be particularly muddy, although usually passable along the edges. Continue downhill and pass a stream bearing away to the right. This is probably the best point for views both up and down the incline, and marks the end of the muddiest stretch.

After another 200 metres, the path crosses a muddy track, and continues (though rather overgrown) to an abrupt end at the Manchester -Wigan railway line. This was opened by the Lancashire and Yorkshire Railway in 1888 and is still in use today. The Bolton to Leigh line crossed here by a bridge which has been demolished, so there is now no access from this point to the line past Atherton. This can be reached separately from Bag Lane at Atherton, including the station site at GR 667038. It is hardly worthwhile as the line, although walkable, is strewn with rubbish, and there is nothing to be seen of the station.

Retrace the route back up the incline, as far as the muddy track. Turn right here on the track, which bisects a former triangular junction for the 1900s extension to Bank Pits 3 and 4. The boggy patch on the left is the site of sidings and the route of the line can be seen about 150 metres along the track. Where it heads left towards Wood End Farm, a line of trees and bushes bearing right marks the colliery extension. Return about halfway to the incline (75 metres) but then turn right across the boggy patch to follow a faint path uphill at the edge of the rough grassland on the left, which leads up to a stile. Cross this and continue up the field, with woodland on the left marking the sites of Bank Pits 1 and 2, to reach a point about 50 metres above the white sign.

Turn left to the sign and stile, where the path right up the incline follows an approximation of the LNWR line, but the actual trackbed becomes increasingly further to the left, as much as 100 metres away in places. It is possible to return by this route, reaching the A6 close by the former LNWR bridge. However the chosen route carries straight on over the incline to follow a track through young woodland to a stile onto a road (Platt Lane). Turn right along the road for 400 metres. By the second bend left, enter a track right at a gate/stile. Here within 50 metres, a gateway gives views up to the buildings of Chequerbent and the former LNWR route in the trees on the skyline. However do **not** go through the gate, instead take the path left immediately before it, between a fence and a hedge. Follow this up to reach a football pitch, with access left to the A58 just below the starting point.

19. Walkden walkabout

Walkden may not be the most obvious of places for a stroll, but this walk combines two quite different lengths of railway line, plus a country park, with some inevitably urban stretches.

Start: Blackleach Country Park, off the A575, half a mile north of the town centre crossroads in Walkden (see inset map). GR 736038.

Distance: 6.3km (almost 4 miles) with only 40 metres (130 ft) height variation.

Map: Pathfinder 712 "Bolton (South)".

By car: Park in the car park at the entrance to the country park from the A575. The access to this is not easily spotted from the A-road. It is best to look out for the prominent spire of the church (St. John the Baptist at Little Hulton) on the western side of the road roughly equidistant (half a mile) from the bridge over the M61 to the north and Walkden town centre to the south. Across the road from the church is a grassy space. At the southern end of this, Hill Top Road leads east. Turn left after 100 metres into John Street, then right into the car park. Note that this clearly indicates gates out are locked at dusk!

By public transport: The only bus services that pass the start are the 25/27 buses between Manchester and Bolton (alight Hill Top Road). Alternatively there are more frequent Manchester-Bolton services, also Manchester-Wigan buses, to Walkden town centre where the route could be joined by the Tesco store off the A6.

The first length of railway walked on this route was not a conventional passengers and freight one but a mineral line built to serve local collieries. These had been served by the underground canal system started in 1759 which led into the Bridgewater Canal at Worsley Delph (see Walk 20). In the middle of the nineteenth century, new mines were developed around Walkden which required the construction of a rail network. The "Linnyshaw Loopline" was part of this network and was constructed in 1865. It was abandoned along with the rest of the colliery network, which included a link to

The "Linnyshaw Loopline" is on the left, passing Blackleach Country Park's reservoir on the right. *(Gordon Suggitt)*

the former Lancashire and Yorkshire Railway at Kearsley, when the mines closed in the 1960s.

The second railway stretch was part of the LNWR line from Roe Green Junction (near Worsley on the line to Tyldesley) to Bolton. This too was originally opened for collieries, this time at Little Hulton in 1870. However demands from local residents for a passenger service led to this being provided five years later. This allowed services from Manchester into Bolton Moor Street, with intermediate stations at Walkden (Low Level or Stocks), Little Hulton and Plodder Lane. Although this route was longer than the LYR line through Clifton Junction, it did have the advantage of a direct link to Manchester London Road (later Piccadilly), allowing through coaches from Bolton to London Euston. Local passenger services however declined markedly after 1945, and ended in 1954. Goods services lasted another seven years, with coal trains from Little Hulton Colliery continuing until 1964. Now the line is walkable right through Walkden from the former Roe Green Junction to the M61, but nothing remains of its stations.

Blackleach Country Park was created in 1991 when, following pressure from local people, Salford purchased land previously designated for housing. Land was reclaimed from the former chemical works on the site and now provides attractive surroundings for the reservoir which once supplied the underground canal network as well as local mills and farms. This was formerly twice its present size as it was cut in two by the Linnyshaw Loopline. The northern half has been drained but the southern part is now the centre piece of the country park.

The Walk

Head out of the far end of the car park and along the southern edge of the reservoir. This is a surprisingly pleasant and airy spot, with views (when clear) north to Winter Hill and the rest of the West Pennine Moors. At the far end of the reservoir, leave by the gate and head left between boulders. Follow the track for 250 metres to a clear junction with the Linnyshaw Loopline. 40 metres ahead, the path bending right on an embankment is on the route of the rail link between the Bridgewater colliery network and the former LYR at Kearsley. (It can be followed through the site of Linnyshaw Moss sidings where the two systems interchanged coal shipments, which is now marked by bridges over the M61 motorway, and on towards Kearsley. Unfortunately the route after this becomes little-walked, and finishes altogether soon after the A666.)

Turn right along the Linnyshaw Loopline which forms a "green corridor" with factories on the right and the M61 over to the left. It is soon on a low but distinct embankment above the once wet land of Linnyshaw Moss. Cross the lane to a garden centre and enter a quite wooded stretch as the path bends right before leading straight to the A6. Past the hedge on the left, landscaped areas lead up to the site of Linnyshaw Colliery in the wooded area above. This was in production by the late 1850s and closed in 1921. Its rail access can be seen going away back left just as the A6 bridge comes into view.

The path swings left alongside the bridge and up to the busy A6. Cross this heading diagonally left to a signpost for "Roe Green Oakwood Recreation Ground". Leave the A6 here and descend

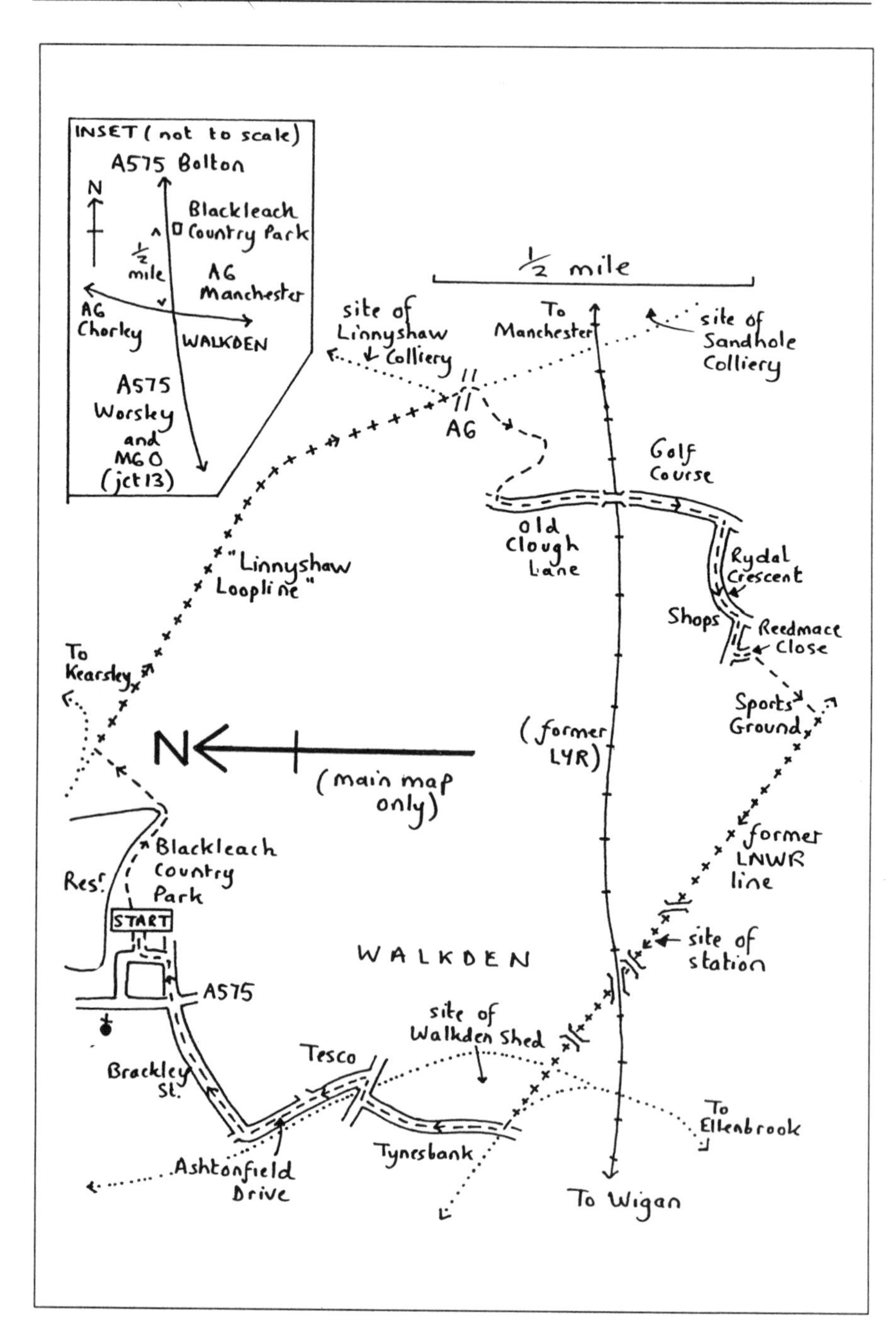

INSET (not to scale)
A575 Bolton
N
Blackleach Country Park
½ mile
A6 Manchester
A6 Chorley
WALKDEN
A575 Worsley and M60 (jct13)
½ mile
site of Linnyshaw Colliery
To Manchester
site of Sandhole Colliery
A6
Golf Course
Old Clough Lane
"Linnyshaw Loopline"
Rydal Crescent
Shops
Reedmace Close
To Kearsley
Sports Ground
N
(main map only)
(former LYR)
former LNWR line
Blackleach Country Park
Res^r
START
site of station
WALKDEN
A575
site of Walkden Shed
Tesco
Brackley St.
To Ellenbrook
Tynesbank
Ashtonfield Drive
To Wigan

wooden steps to fork right at a wrecked signpost. Go down more steps to the footbridge and continue with the stream on the left. This area is How Clough Woods, which is particularly attractive when the bluebells are in flower. (This is not part of the rail route which continued past Sandhole (Bridgewater) Colliery – now part of Ellesmere Golf Course – en route for Worsley.) The path bears right up more steps to a gate into a recreation ground. Head diagonally across this to bins by an exit to a road (Old Clough Lane). Turn left down this to cross the still-used Manchester-Wigan (former LYR) line. Passing the golf clubhouse on the left, take the next right into Rydal Crescent. Follow this round to the fourth exit on the right, just after the row of shops. Turn right here and almost immediately left into Reedmace Close. As this swings left, go straight on past concrete pillars and across the sports ground to reach the former railway in the trees ahead.

Turn right onto the former line to Bolton (Moor Street). After an uneventful stretch, this is crossed by four bridges in quick succession. The first of these is for Walkden Road (A575), adorned with signal-type signs. Just past this is the site of Walkden's LNWR station, where nothing is left but a vandalised information board. Next is Park Road bridge, followed by the massive bridge for the current Manchester-Wigan railway line and lastly Bridgewater Road bridge. 100 metres after this, on the right between a factory and housing there is the brick abutment of the former Bridgewater Collieries line. This ran south from Ashton's Field and Ellesmere mines at Walkden to the former LNWR Manchester -Wigan line at Ellenbrook and the Bridgewater Canal at Booth's Bank. After another 120 metres, a clear path swings to join from the left; this was a connection to the collieries line. Ignore this and continue to the right-hand set of steps ahead; go up these to the street called Tynesbank.

Across the road the line of the former railway resumes and can be followed past the A6, but turn right instead and proceed up Tynesbank. On the right, where new housing now stands, was the location of "Walkden Shed". This was the main maintenance depot for the whole Bridgewater Collieries rail system, and continued in business after the closure of that system in 1970, only finally closing down in 1986. Continue up Tynesbank to the A6, noting the fine

"Brougham House 1880" date stone on the left and the almost-hidden Tynesbank Old Farm to the right. At the A6 turn right over the bridge which was built over the collieries line but now has traffic for the shopping centre under it instead! Cross the A6 at the end of the bridge and turn left, keeping the Tesco superstore on the right. As the access road swings in from the left, keep straight on along Ashtonfield Drive. Through the gaps between houses on the left, their gardens can be seen where the line to Ashton's Field Colliery once ran. Follow the road round right into Brackley Street which leads up to the A575 across from Hill Top Road and the starting point.

20. By the first canal?

Worsley

The former public railway here is overshadowed in historical importance by the nearby Bridgewater Canal. Both are walked on this route, with a look at Worsley – still attractive despite the M60!

Start: The car park off the B5211, across the road from Worsley Court House. GR 747004.

Distance: 5.4km (three and one-third miles) on almost level terrain.

Map: Most of the route is on Pathfinder 712 "Bolton (South)". A small portion is on the next sheet to the south, Pathfinder 723 "Eccles (Greater Manchester)", but this section shouldn't provide any navigational difficulties.

By car: The car park is on the south side of the eastern roundabout for access to/from the M60 at junction 13 and the A572 and A575. Take the B5211 (Eccles) exit from the roundabout; the entrance to the car park is within 50 yards on the right.

By public transport: There are frequent bus services to Worsley (Court House) from Leigh, Wigan, Bolton and Manchester.

To explain the questionmark in the title, the Bridgewater Canal was preceded, even within north-west England, by the Sankey Canal at St. Helens, part of which opened in 1757. However the Bridgewater could fairly be described as the first **major** canal in Britain. Engineered by James Brindley for Francis Egerton, 3rd Duke of Bridgewater, it was built between 1759 and 1765 to transport coal from the duke's mines at Worsley to Castlefield in Manchester. Worsley Delph, close to the start of the walk, is the most visible remnant of the early coal-carrying days of the canal. Two entrances lead into the underground section of the canal system, started in 1759. Eventually there were 40 to 50 miles (estimates vary) of narrow underground canals on separate levels linked by an incline under Walkden. A million tons of coal a year passed through these caverns until the 1860s, when the development of new collieries led to the construction of a surface rail system (see Walk 19). Even then a major outlet for the colliery rail system was at Worsley Basin, half a mile along the surface canal towards Monton. Use of the canal for passenger traffic can also be seen with the Packet House (1760). Here tickets were bought for the passenger boats to Runcorn and Manchester, reached down the adjacent Boat Steps. Like the underground canal system, passenger services largely ended with the arrival of the railways in the 1860s.

Rail passenger and freight services reached Worsley with the opening of the LNWR Eccles to Wigan line in 1864. Worsley was provided with commuter access to Manchester, and services west to Wigan, Leigh and Liverpool. There were Bolton to Manchester trains via Walkden, and even via Chequerbent and Tyldesley. This latter service somehow survived until 1942, but the following decades saw the steady loss of all services to Worsley, finishing with the closure of the Eccles-Wigan line in 1969. Worsley was not the only station on the section of line walked here, as one was added in 1887 at Monton Green for commuters to Manchester. It was built on a bridge that often proved too low for road traffic, so that it was probably a relief when it too closed in 1969 and the bridge (plus station) demolished. The Eccles-Wigan line is walkable in this area from Monton Green (the furthest point of this walk) through Worsley and Roe Green to Ellenbrook (GR 726018). For west of Ellenbrook, see Walk 17. In addition, to the east of Worsley village there was a major link of the Bridgewater Collieries railway system, from the mines at Walkden to Worsley Basin on the Bridgewater Canal. It was thus a continuation of the "Linnyshaw Loopline" dealt with in Walk 19. The stretch from the former LNWR line to the A575 is walkable and is included here.

Just as the 3rd Duke of Bridgewater was responsible for the industrial importance of Worsley, its appearance today is largely the legacy of his great-nephew, the 1st Earl of Ellesmere. His construction of buildings such as the Court House and Boathouse, and the attractive half-timbering of others such as the Packet House give the village its charm still evident today. Details are provided on the five information boards visited on the walk, and are covered by leaflets such as Salford's "The Worsley Village Heritage Trail" and so will only be mentioned here.

The coal tip at Worsley Basin in 1957. Here, coal from Walkden's collieries via the Linnyshaw Loopline was loaded onto barges on the Bridgewater Canal. *(C.H.A. Townley)*

The Walk

Head back to the car park's entrance, noting information board 1 on the right. Cross the road diagonally right to go down to the canal by the florist's. Information board 2 is directly above the Boat Steps, while further down the canal can be seen the Oil Store of 1854 – now apartments – and the Boathouse. Turn left to pass the Packet House and cross the "Alphabet Bridge" to the Nailmaker's House, built about 1725 and thus predating the canal. Go left of this building up shallow steps to reach the A572. Crossing the road diagonally left leads to the bridge parapet overlooking Worsley Delph. Here the two exits from the underground canal system can clearly be seen, with a 1930s replica of one of the boats used half-sunk in the orange-coloured water. Information board 3 is to the right of the site, but there is currently (mid-1998) no access into the Delph.

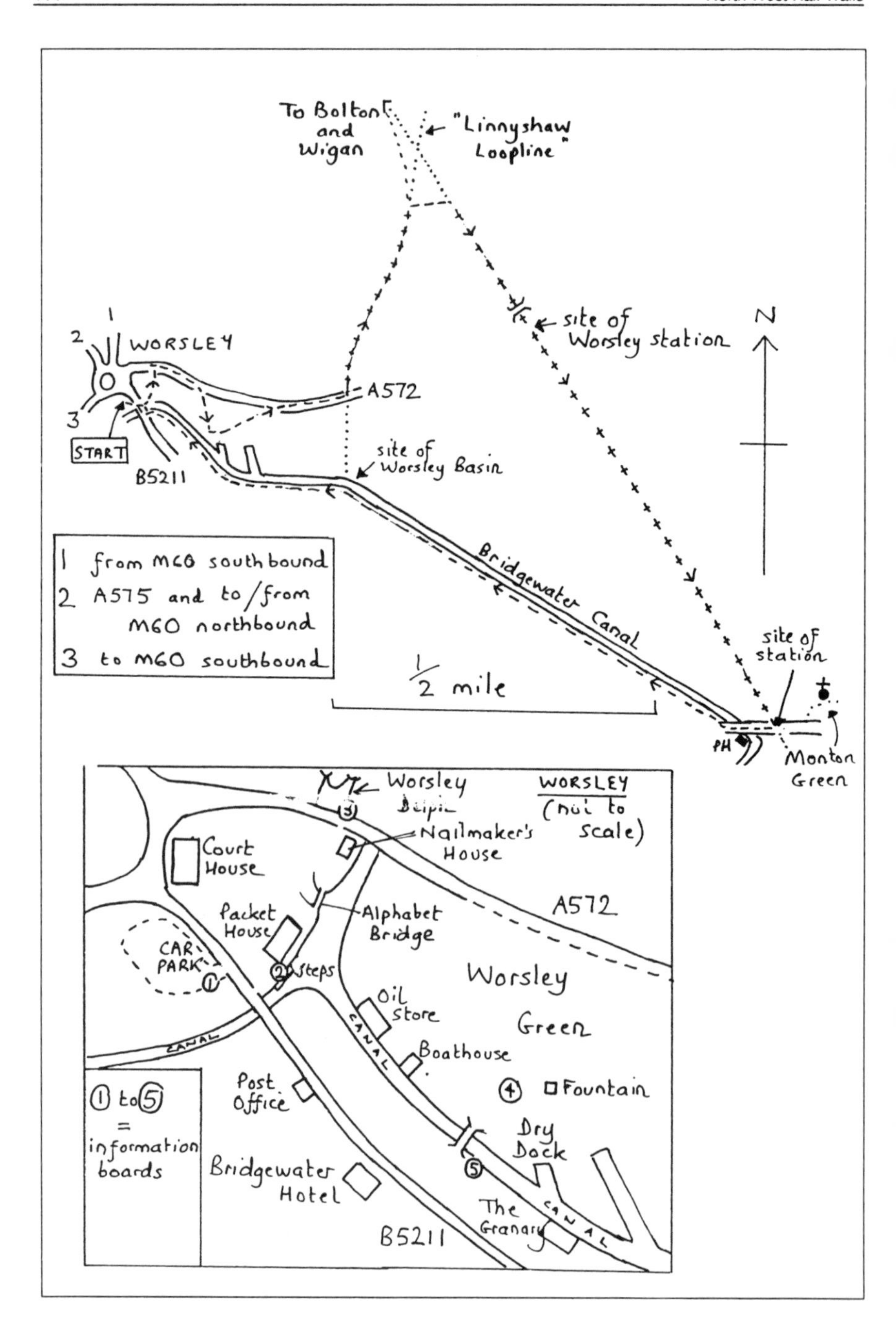
To Bolton and Wigan
"Linnyshaw Loopline"
site of Worsley station
N
1
2
3
WORSLEY
A572
START
B5211
site of Worsley Basin
Bridgewater Canal
1 from M60 southbound
2 A575 and to/from M60 northbound
3 to M60 southbound
1/2 mile
site of station
PH
Monton Green
Worsley
WORSLEY
(not to Scale)
Nailmaker's House
Court House
A572
Packet House
Alphabet Bridge
CAR PARK
Steps
Worsley Green
Oil store
CANAL
CANAL
Boathouse
Post Office
Fountain
① to ⑤ = information boards
Dry Dock
Bridgewater Hotel
The Granary
CANAL
B5211

Turn back along the A572 towards Swinton passing the Nailmaker's House to reach Worsley Green. It is hard now to envisage this green oasis as the industrial complex it was up to about 1903. Walk across the right-hand side of the Green to reach information board 4, then left to the "Fountain" – a memorial to the 3rd Duke of Bridgewater constructed from the base of the Works Yard chimney! Head left across the Green to its far corner and continue along the A572. In about 250 metres, as the road swings left, go left to leave it at railings and Public Footpath signs. This is the track of the former Bridgewater Collieries line to Worsley Basin. Just past the school grounds, ignore the steps left and keep right, almost under the power lines. At a gate, leave the mineral line (which carried straight on to the LNWR line and the Walkden mines) and descend right to the track of the LNWR Eccles-Wigan line on the stretch called the "Tyldesley Loopline" for recreational purposes.

Turn right onto the track and head towards Monton in a deep cutting. Just after the bridge for Worsley Road with its railway-style signs is the site of Worsley station. This still has platforms, plus seats and an information board. Next along the track is a long straight stretch in a setting almost totally rural despite the hum of motorway traffic, though the countryside to the left soon becomes a golf course. This length ends abruptly with an information board for Monton Green station (of which no trace remains) and a descent to Parrin Lane. It is worth walking a few metres left to view the Green overlooked by the Unitarian church of 1875.

The main route heads right along Parrin Lane to the bridge over the canal. Almost built into this is the southern lodge (gatehouse) for Duke's Drive. This was a carriage drive leading almost a mile north through the 1st Earl of Ellesmere's estate. Cross the bridge and turn right down to the towpath. Just the other side of the bridge is the Barge Inn, at an almost right-angled bend in the canal. (This is where the canal's route was changed from its original destination of Salford to a crossing of the Irwell at Barton en route for Castlefield in Manchester.) However the route for this walk means heading back along the towpath towards Worsley, whose church steeple is soon in view. After a long straight stretch, just as the canal bends left under power lines, there is a reed-filled gap in the canal bank at the right. This is all that is left of Worsley Basin, where the Bridgewater Collieries railway reached the canal for outward coal shipments. Now the sites of canal arms and rail sidings are all occupied by modern housing.

The canal, usually lined with boats at the right, now enters Worsley passing the original Dry Docks of around 1760 – the oldest still working on Britain's inland waterways. Just before the footbridge on the towpath side is the Granary – once a water-powered forge, now offices – also the fifth and last Worsley information board. After the footbridge over on the left is the B5211 (Barton Road) with the Bridgewater Hotel (1903) and shops including post office and tea room. This can be followed back to the start, or alternatively the canal can be followed round past the Duke's Boathouse (1851), Oil Store and Packet House (all on the far bank) to pass under Worsley Bridge. Immediately past the bridge, steps left lead up to the B5211. A left turn leads over the bridge and back to the car park.

21. Rails to Ringley Road

Outwood

Trains no longer go to Ringley Road station, but public access should now be better than in recent years due to developments such as the re-opened bridge over the Irwell and improvements to the former rail route as far as the M60..

Start: The bridge on the A667 Kearsley-Whitefield road as it crosses the former railway line at GR 775056.

Distance: 5km (just over 3 miles) on mostly level terrain, although there is a steady climb of about 40 metres (130ft) up from the Irwell on the return journey.

Map: Pathfinder 712 "Bolton (South)".

By car: Coming from Kearsley, there is a large car park on the left by workshops, about 100 metres after the bridge and the "Ringley Car Sales" garage. This is about 250 metres after the houses at Outwood village for those travelling in the opposite direction.

By public transport: There are regular services between Bolton and Whitefield or Radcliffe/Bury (via Outwood). Bus stops are immediately west of the bridge, at the end of Wood Street.

This walk again uses the line built by the East Lancashire Railway, opened in 1846. The stretch walked here was part of the six miles of track from Clifton Junction on the Lancashire and Yorkshire Railway to Bury which began with a thirteen-arch viaduct over the Irwell. This was followed by a lengthy climb at 1 in 96 up to Ringley Road (the present A667), then a descent back to the Irwell at Radcliffe, and a final climb to Bury. Originally the only intermediate station was at Radcliffe Bridge, but Ringley Road was added in 1847 and Molyneux Brow in 1853. The first addition was isolated between the small settlements of Ringley and Outwood, but Molyneux Brow was truly in the middle of nowhere! Not surprisingly, it closed as early as 1931. Ringley Road's closure came in 1953 followed by

Radcliffe Bridge in 1958, both well before the whole line as far as Radcliffe North Junction in 1966.

The line is still walkable from the northern end of the Clifton viaduct to the Radcliffe crossing of the Irwell, and should now be improved from its former often very wet and muddy condition. There is a gap for the M60 motorway (crossed by a footbridge now re-located on the line of the railway), which has also claimed the site of Molyneux Brow station. Radcliffe Bridge station site has also been lost to road developments, leaving Ringley Road as the only station with any remains today.

Also visited is the Manchester, Bolton and Bury Canal, opened in 1796 to link these three towns with 15 miles of waterway. From Manchester, fifteen locks were used to gain 187 feet in height up to two level stretches joining Bolton and Bury. Although its passenger services were soon lost to the railways, the canal remained prosperous through local industries (coal, cotton and chemicals) right up to a disastrous breach close to the start of the Bury stretch in 1936. This was followed by the draining of much of the locks portion during World War 2 (to reduce the risk of flooding from bomb damage). Only the Bury stretch remained busy until the late 1940s, when its last main user, the colliery at Ladyshore, closed. The canal was sold off and fell into disrepair, but in 1987 a society was formed which aims to restore the canal to use. This would be a simple task along the stretch walked here which is still in water although overgrown, but the lower portion is mostly filled-in and the last part of the Bolton section is now a dual-carriageway.

There have been enormous recent changes along the Outwood-Radcliffe section of the route. At the Outwood end these have centred on the former colliery site which has been landscaped as a setting for a major work of sculpture. A set of monolithic slabs of Spanish granite by the sculptor Ulrich Ruckriem was originally part of "artstranspennine 98", but now is included in the Irwell Sculpture Trail. Between this site and the Irwell, the former railway line has been redeveloped for use by walkers, horse-riders and the disabled, and at the crossing of the Irwell the 1882 LYR railway bridge has been restored to its former glory and re-opened to pedestrians.

The downside to these major improvement schemes is that the

landscaping has been so extensive that almost all trace of the area's former industries has been lost. Chief amongst these was Outwood Colliery, 1865 to 1931, which employed 2,000 at its peak when it was also extracting coal from two other pits alongside the railway to the NE. To the south, by the A667, were brickworks, and further north, across the railway, short-lived iron works operated towards the end of last century. There was also a power station closer to the Irwell. This operated from 1905 to 1960 and was served by sidings from the railway leading to narrow-gauge inclines down into the boilers. Now almost nothing is left of all this industrial activity.

Outwood Colliery, shown here in 1913, once employed 2,000 but is now just a landscaped grassy area. *(J. Ryan collection)*

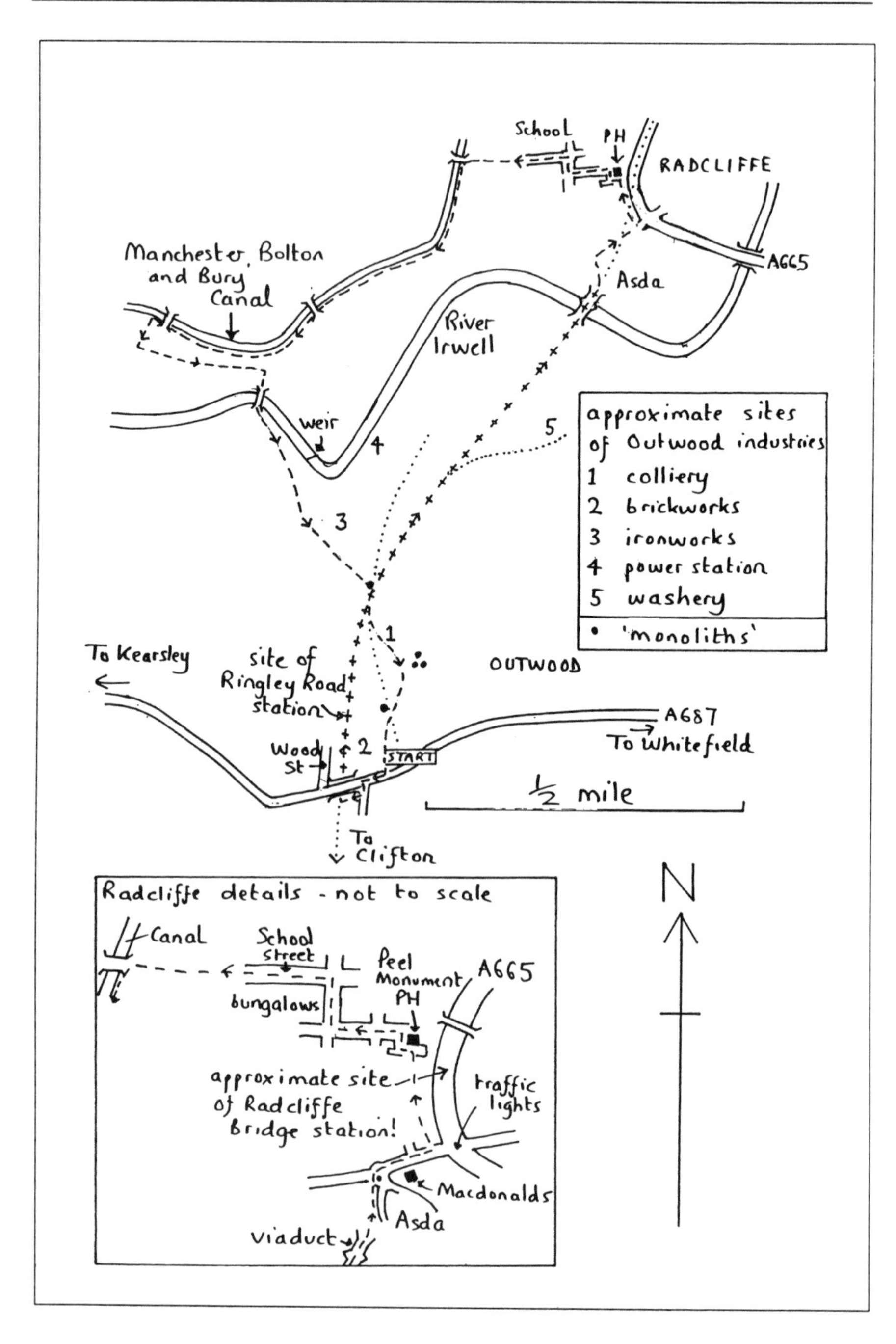
School
PH
RADCLIFFE
Manchester, Bolton and Bury Canal
A665
Asda
River Irwell
weir
4
3
5
approximate sites of Outwood industries
1 colliery
2 brickworks
3 ironworks
4 power station
5 washery
• 'monoliths'
1
To Kearsley
site of Ringley Road station
OUTWOOD
A687
To Whitefield
Wood St
2
START
½ mile
To Clifton
Radcliffe details - not to scale
Canal
School Street
Peel Monument PH
A665
bungalows
approximate site of Radcliffe Bridge station!
traffic lights
Macdonalds
Asda
viaduct
N

The Walk

Walk from the car park back to the main road and turn right towards Kearsley. Cross at the garage left into the lane for Lower Heap Stables. Almost immediately, a stile on the right gives access down steps to the railway. It is worth pausing to examine the road bridge whose size and extensive brickwork cannot be gauged from the road above. Turn right on the former trackbed under the bridge to the site of Ringley Road station, still with its northbound platform, plus seats and a commemorative plaque. Continue along the trackbed to reach the largest of the stone monoliths, placed where the path from the rest of the sculpture site reaches the former railway line. Hereabouts the lines from the colliery, brickworks and power station joined the "main" line (see map). Continue along the trackbed towards Radcliffe, here occupied by a grey shaly path. Just after a pebbly path has joined from the left, another path heads off right. This roughly follows lines that led to the colliery washery which continued in use long after the colliery closed, dealing with coal from Astley Green and Pendlebury until final closure in 1956. Continue on the former railway as it swings gently right then left to reach the restored Outwood Viaduct.

Once across the viaduct, take the ramp down to the mini-roundabout at the entrance to Asda. Bear right here, keeping Macdonalds on the right and passing a road to the left to almost reach the traffic lights. Just before the lights, a path heads left up the slope towards the Peel Monument pub. This crosses the route of the former railway as it headed towards the site of Radcliffe Bridge station, now replaced by the A665! Pass the pub on the right and turn left into the road on its far side, then along to bungalows where a right turn leads to School Street. Turn left here, keeping the school on the right. Keep straight on as the road becomes unsurfaced to reach the canal at a footbridge. Do not cross this but drop to the canal towpath near a pipe-bridge. Turn left on the towpath which is followed for about 1100 metres (almost three-quarters of a mile).

The canal, still in water but filled with reeds and rushes which provide a haven for waterbirds, soon heads out into open country with views back left to the railway bridge. Continue under the next canal bridge with a large modern factory on the far side, passing the

M (Manchester) 9½ (miles) stone and then brick-built houses. Just past these, there is a view down to the Irwell at a weir. The M9¼ stone comes next, just before a length of brick wall built by the canal company to enclose the grounds of Mount Sion House. 50 metres after the next bridge, there is a clear gap in this wall. Go through this to a broad path leading down towards the Irwell at a white house where it reaches a roughly surfaced road. Turn left on this and walk through woodland, fenced-off on the right. Soon there is an open bracken slope on the left leading up to the brick embankment supporting the canal on the stretch just walked.

Now watch out for a clear (and official) gap in the forbidding wire fence on the right. This allows access to a footbridge over the Irwell, after which a clear path bears left and up the hillside. The Irwell can usually be heard roaring over the weir seen earlier. A short path left through the bracken allows a clearer view of this, with the overgrown site of the power station on the far side of the river bend. Continue up the main path, ignoring a stile into the clearly landscaped fields on the right. Just before the path goes below power lines, mounds of slag can be seen over on the left, all that is left of the ironworks. Continue past the Irwell Valley Way sign to the monolith seen on the outward journey.

This time turn right onto the railway but then left away from it on a tarmac path heading up newly landscaped slopes. Towards the top of the slope look back for a fine view (if clear) to the West Pennine Moors including Winter Hill (with the TV masts) and Holcombe's Peel Tower. The seven smaller monoliths which form the main group of sculptures now appear on the left. These mark the main site of Outwood Colliery, but the paths around them are shaly and glutinous after rain so it is better to keep to the tarmac as it swings away to the right, passing a further monolith, to reach the car park at the start of the walk.

22. East of Oldham

Grotton – Lees

This is not quite "East of Eden", but the hilly eastern outskirts of Oldham provide a surprisingly varied setting for this walk along the line that once led out to Saddleworth.

Start: The former station at Grotton, off the A669 at GR 964043.

Distance: 5.5km (almost 3½ miles) with 65 metres (210 ft) of height gain.

Map: Pathfinder 713 "Oldham".

By car: Grotton is about two and a half miles east of Oldham town centre on the A669 Oldham-Greenfield (Saddleworth) road. Turn right at the Grotton pub in the centre of the settlement into Station Road which after 250 metres curves right into a car park.

By public transport: There are frequent bus services from Oldham along Lees Road to Grotton. Alight at the Grotton pub and walk down Station Road to the start of the walk.

The branch to Greenfield was Oldham's second railway and was opened by the LNWR in 1856, five years after the line to Delph. Through trains were thus able to run from a temporary station at Oldham Mumps (by the Lancashire and Yorkshire Railway station still in use today) to Delph. On the Greenfield section there were intermediate stations at Lees, where an engine shed was built in 1878, and Grotton. In 1862 the Mumps terminus was replaced by a new station at Oldham Glodwick Road, and in 1912 a halt was added at Grasscroft west of Greenfield. The major engineering work on the line was the Lydgate tunnel, three-quarters of a mile long, leading to the Tame valley.

The line became heavily used by Oldham commuters so that by the First World War there were 36 trains each way per day. However it was paralleled by the present-day A669 so that custom was soon lost to trams (as far as Lees) and later buses and cars. Passenger services ended in 1955 and goods trains nine years later, when the line closed including the engine shed at Lees. East of Grotton station, the trackbed is soon overgrown leading to the sealed-off Lydgate tunnel. From Grotton westwards the route is walkable right into Oldham, but the section west of Lees is designated a "linear park" so it becomes increasingly landscaped (and in places litter-strewn). All evidence of the station at Glodwick Road and the connections through to Clegg Street has been lost.

A Oldham-Delph train near Grotton before the end of passenger services in 1955. *(J. Davenport)*

The Walk

From the car park walk back to the last house at the bottom of Station Road. This is the former Grotton station-master's house, now a private residence and looking very different from views of it at the end of railway operations in 1964. It is worth walking along the surviving platform across from the house, but not beyond it as the trackbed soon disappears in dense undergrowth leading to the blocked-up western end of Lydgate tunnel.

Retrace the route back to Station Road, and cross it to a path parallel to the car park on the left. This approximately follows the rail line but the area has been extensively landscaped, including the site of the station goods shed over on the left. The path swings right above the rooftop of a cottage tucked in a hollow where once stood Radcliffe Mill, before following a more obvious route of the trackbed between modern housing as it ascends to a filled-in road bridge. Cross this and proceed to the busy A669. Here the bridge has also been filled in, but the far side's bridgework is clear over on the left as the road is crossed (with care) to the end of Station Street. Here the path drops back down left to regain the railway just below the former bridge. Continue through more modern housing, until a straight stretch towards a remaining bridge gives more of an impression of a railway. This is the site of Lees station of which nothing remains, including the engine shed which was over to the right, although the access road to the former station can still be seen coming in at the left.

Pass under the bridge with a strangely rocket-like cemetery chapel on the hillside ahead. Views soon become hidden by trees, though as the line is now on an embankment there are glimpses of surviving mills on the left. As the line swings left over a wooded valley, the views open out to Hartshead Pike with its tower and, if clear, the western edges of the Pennines past Macclesfield, before a drop to a road marks the end of the railway section of this walk.

Turn left on the road (Wellyhole Street) and walk along to the A669. Cross the main road diagonally left to pick up a path on the far side bearing right into bushes, with the imposing Lees Brook Mill over on the left. Keep straight on the path as it crosses a stepped path to go alongside a stone wall on the right. Keep straight on past a yel-

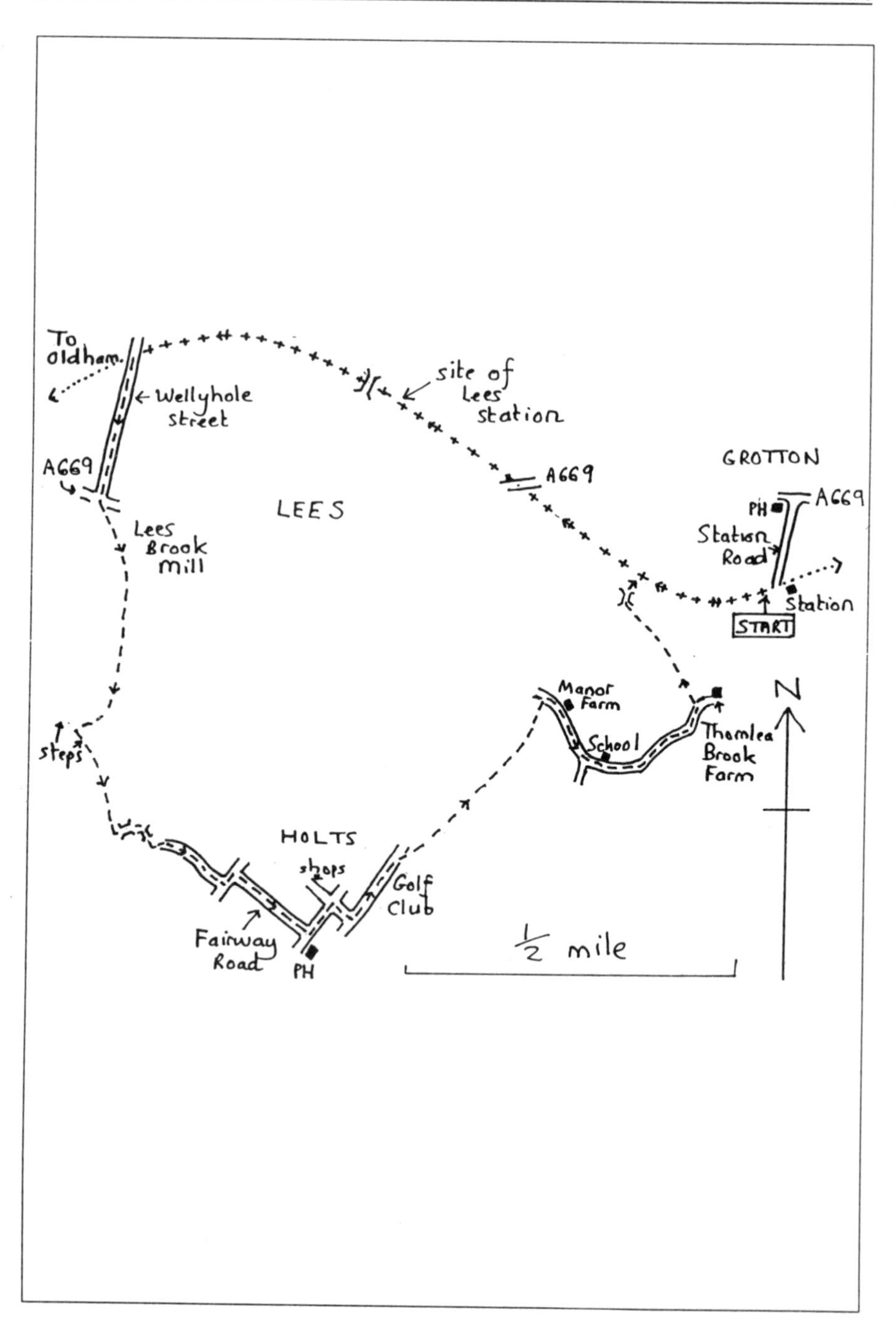
To Oldham
Wellyhole Street
site of Lees station
A669
GROTTON
LEES
A669
PH
A669
Station Road
Lees Brook Mill
Station
START
Manor Farm
School
Thornlea Brook Farm
N
steps
HOLTS
shops
Golf Club
Fairway Road
PH
1/2 mile

low marker post and down a few steps to reach an open valley floor. Follow this path along the left edge of the valley floor, ignoring all paths left and right, until the path swings right to join a concreted path just below steps up to the right. Turn left instead towards Hartshead Pike and descend steps back down to the valley bottom. Follow the path just below a spur on the left, with the stream now visible below it, to reach a rough track at a "Medlock Valley Breeze Hill" sign. Turn left on the track and over the stream on a metal footbridge. As the track forks, bear right over a second footbridge, and then left up steps to reach modern houses.

Go straight ahead on the road through the modern houses, and turn left then right into Fairway Road. At the end of this road, with the Red Rose Inn visible to the right, turn left and along to the next crossroads, with an interesting view of the estate shops on the left! Turn right and then left alongside the golf course. Just past the Club House, a "Bridle Path" sign points right onto a track. Follow this as it heads away from and slightly above the estate to give extensive views over the eastern areas of Oldham. Pass attractive stone houses then more modern residences before the track drops to a road.

Turn right on this rather narrow lane watching out for traffic, which although sparse does not leave much room for walkers on this stretch! Pass Knowls Lane Farm and Manor Farm before forking left at a junction to pass the school and Flash Cottages. Ignore a broad entrance right to Kiln Farm and head left along the narrow walled lane. Here views are extensive across the valley on the left, including glimpses of the rail route, and there is a fine prospect towards Lydgate church high on the ridge which is tunnelled through by the railway en route for Greenfield.

At a sharp right bend just **before** Thornlea Brook Farm, an anonymous signpost points left down the hillside. Leave the lane here and proceed down the field, keeping a line of telegraph poles just to the left. At the bottom of the slope, cross a stile to a wooden footbridge. To the right of this there used to be a reservoir for once-extensive mills on the left. Go over the bridge, cross another stile and go up steps to paths at the top, where a right turn brings the route onto the landscaped area leading back to the car park.

23. Industrial Revolution remnant

Park Bridge

The North-West's "Coalbrookdale" forms the centrepiece for this walk by railway and canal in the rural setting of the Medlock Valley yet only two miles from the centre of Oldham.

Start: Park Bridge Visitor Centre. GR 940025.

Distance: 7.3km (4½ miles) with much level terrain although there are some short sharp climbs, especially around Park Bridge. The length can be reduced by 1km by a short cut at Daisy Nook or by nearly 2km by using a 350 metres stretch of the A627 but both these miss much of interest from the canal part of the walk (see map). **Note:** The railway section of the walk is one of the least maintained in this book with a rather overgrown stretch in the middle and three missing bridges necessitating quite a scramble up and down from the trackbed (though most of this can be avoided by a detour past Wester Hill). There are also more muddy stretches than usual though the worst of these (Bardsley Bridge to Fennyfield) is also avoidable.

Map: Pathfinder 713 "Oldham".

By car: Park Bridge is sign-posted off the A627 between Oldham and Ashton-under-Lyne. Park across from the Visitor Centre. Note that the car park closes at 5pm.

By public transport: There are no buses to Park Bridge but the walk can be reached from Bardsley Bridge on the A627 where there are regular bus services between Oldham and Ashton-under-Lyne.

Park Bridge is considered to be the oldest surviving industrial community in the North West based on engineering rather than textiles. Its story began in 1784 when Samuel Lees converted a water driven corn mill to manufacture rollers for spinning mills in the growing cotton industry. A century later new engineering shops were built further east, the remains of which can still be seen, along with much of the village. The first transport for the works was by canal and tram

The scene at Park Bridge today, from the railway embankment. *(Gordon Suggitt)*

road. A branch of the Ashton Canal led north from Droylsden to Daisy Nook (now a Country Park) in the Medlock Valley. There it split with one branch going NW to Hollinwood, the other NE towards Park Bridge. However the terminus was at Fennyfield Bridge, half a mile short of the works. Thus in about 1800, a 3ft 6in gauge tram road was opened to link the works to the canal. Originally horse-drawn, small locos were later used before closure around 1880.

A conventional rail link arrived in 1861 with the opening of the Oldham, Ashton-under-Lyne and Guide Bridge Junction Railway, which was soon operated jointly by the LNWR and the Manchester, Sheffield and Lincolnshire Railway. Starting at a new station in Oldham, Clegg Street, the line linked the places in its title, with the only station outside them at Park Bridge, where there was also a nine-arch viaduct and a line into the eastern end of the works. Clegg Street became Oldham's principal station and the line more than just a branch, with services to Manchester and even London King's

Cross. Local passenger services however were hard hit by competition from trams and later buses linking the towns, but survived until 1959. Goods trains lasted till 1967, Park Bridge works having closed six years earlier. The former line is walkable for much of its length between Oldham and Ashton-under-Lyne, though north of Park Bridge much of it is covered by tarmac, while south of the stretch in this walk litter becomes an increasing problem.

The Walk

Across the road from the car park is the Visitor Centre which is open 12 noon to 4pm Wednesday and Thursday, 11am to 5pm Saturday, Sunday and Bank Holidays (10-4 in winter). This contains a wealth of information, especially on Park Bridge itself, so only a brief mention of the buildings passed on this walk will be given here.

From the car park, built on the Upper Roller Shed of 1889, and the Visitor Centre based in the 1860s stables, walk up the very rough lane passing on the left Dingle Terrace, the Institute (1863), the site of the church (now modern housing) and Dean Terrace. On the right are the modernized Coach House and Dean House, built for the Lees family in 1844. At the end of Dean Terrace, turn right down the narrow tarmac lane as it drops steeply past Mill Brow Cottage (once the works manager's house). A sharp right turn brings the lane alongside the main part of the works, the Bottom Forge, on the right, with a stone embankment approaching from the left. This carried the works branch line which formerly bridged the lane into the forge. Just past this on the left are the brick foundations of the 1860s gas works, then the bridge over the Medlock. Just past this on the right is the sadly bricked-up former post office, closed in 1994. Looking the other way, upstream, the path on the right of the stream is the route of the tramway from Fennyfield Bridge as it emerged from a tunnel under the works and continued up the valley to the pits in Rocher Vale.

Take the track to the **left** of the stream. This is at first roughly paved with slag but then with stone blocks as the edge of the former Upper Forge is crossed. Keep to the right of an open grassy patch to pick up a line of wooden sleepers. This is the route of the works branch line from Park Bridge station (previously seen at the embankment by Bottom Forge). It can be followed through a quarry and over a rickety wooden bridge (used by the railway). The ruined building on the left was a pump house for the Rocher Pit, part of the remains of the once-extensive coal mining industry of the area. The path, still with plenty of wooden sleepers, swings right after the bridge to cross the line of the tramway and climb an incline above the opposite bank of the Medlock. There is a break for a lane, but carry straight on up the slope. The actual rail route now becomes overgrown, the path keeping just left of it to a T-junction. To the right was a siding heading towards the former station master's house (now part of a kennels/cattery) and straight ahead would have been Park Bridge station. There is still a wood and stone structure in the undergrowth – perhaps a loading bay.

Turn left following the wooden sleepers of the works branch as it curves to meet the "main" line on a bracken-covered bank coming in from the right. Once on this line, the path soon forks either side of a missing bridge. It is best to take the left-hand option down to the tarmac where a decision has to be made. It is possible to head up the far side back onto the embankment and continue towards Ashton. However the path is narrow and is becoming overgrown for a stretch. In addition there are two more missing bridges, and the first gap involves quite a steep scramble down and back onto the line. (Once past this, the path is less overgrown and the final missing bridge causes less of a problem.) The alternative is to head down the lane for 100 metres, then bear left into the drive for Wester Hill (the Lees family home from 1886). Turn left approaching the buildings, through a gate and stile, and back to the railway keeping to the edge of the field on the left.

Either way the route is back on the railway line before the deep wooded cleft of Holden Clough, where the bridge (more a culvert through an embankment) is still intact. At the end, as new housing approaches, turn right at a "½ ml Oldham Road" sign. Pass under power lines and alongside a fence on the left separating the path from new houses. Keep straight on as the path becomes a track through the farmyard at Limehurst and out onto a ridge with views ahead to Manchester city centre's office blocks. A little further on,

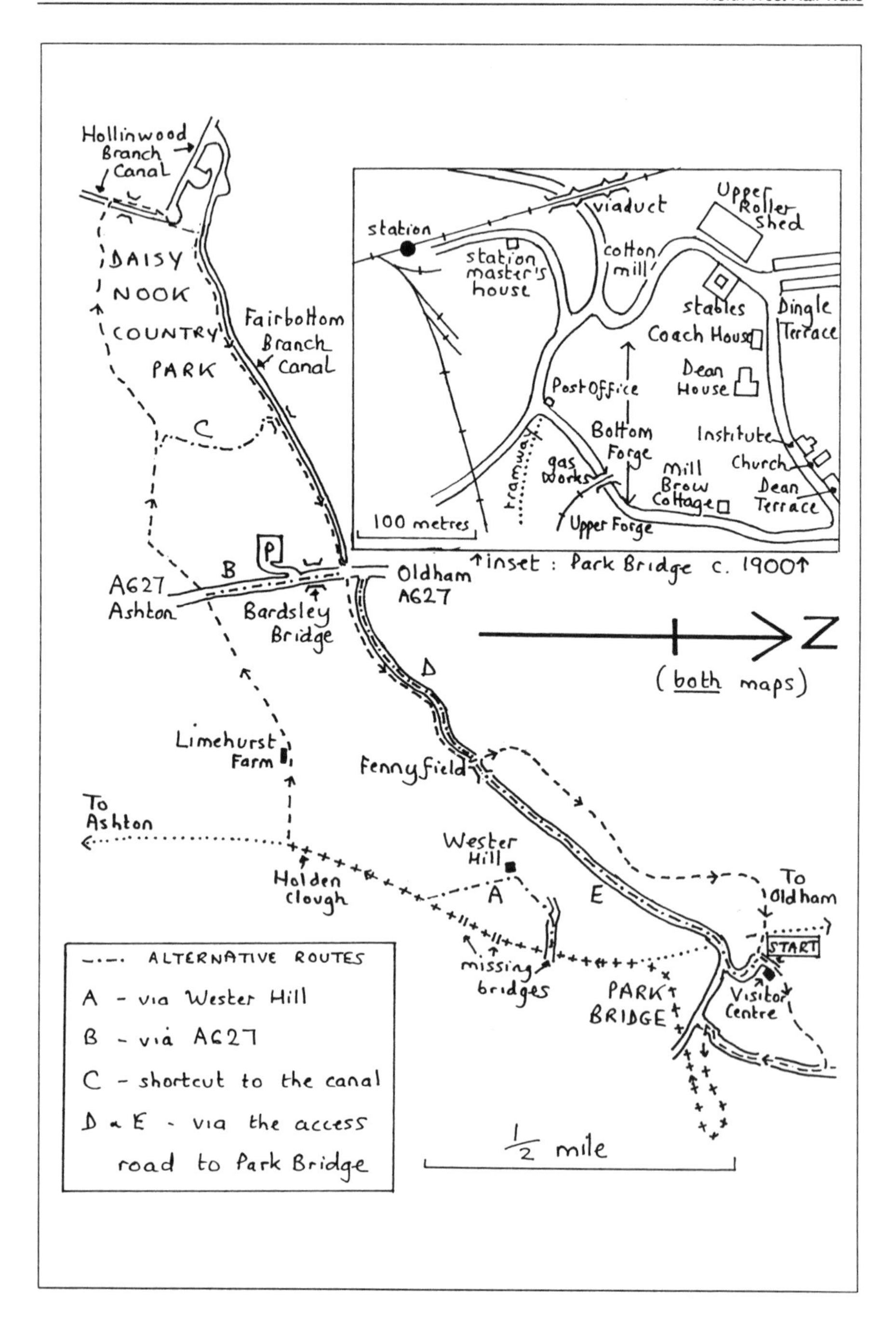
Hollinwood Branch Canal
DAISY NOOK COUNTRY PARK
Fairbottom Branch Canal
C
P
B
A627 Ashton
Bardsley Bridge
Oldham A627
D
Limehurst Farm
Fennyfield
To Ashton
Wester Hill
Holden Clough
A
E
missing bridges
PARK BRIDGE
To Oldham
START
Visitor Centre
station
viaduct
Upper Roller Shed
station master's house
cotton mill
stables
Dingle Terrace
Coach House
Dean House
Post Office
Bottom Forge
Institute
Church
gas works
tramway
Mill Brow Cottage
Dean Terrace
Upper Forge
100 metres
inset : Park Bridge c. 1900
N
(both maps)
ALTERNATIVE ROUTES
A - via Wester Hill
B - via A627
C - shortcut to the canal
D & E - via the access road to Park Bridge
1/2 mile

the view extends almost through 360° including back towards the Pennines, before the farm road dips to pass a wood on the right shortly before reaching the main road (A627). Here the first of two possible shortenings of the walk involves walking right along the busy road to Bardsley Bridge (see map).

However the full route crosses the road diagonally right to a "¼ ml Daisy Nook Country Park" sign. Head up the track here back to the power lines, then just before a bend right, another finger-post points right across the field indicating a clear path. This becomes paved for a stretch before heading for another signpost visible a long way ahead. This marks a second alternative shortcut (turning right down to the Medlock and up to the canal), but the full route continues straight on with a fence to the left and woods on the right. After dropping slightly into the woods for a spell, the path regains the fence line for a lengthy stretch which ends at a roughly paved drop through the woods to steps down to the canal. This is the Hollinwood Branch Canal, reached as it emerged from the former Boodle Tunnel on the left (opened-up in the 1920s). Cross it and turn right along the towpath on an aqueduct over the Medlock (a popular spot on summer Sundays). Next is a crudely filled-in lock, the first of four raising the canal 15 metres to its top level, then a weed-covered pond. This was a turning basin needed for long narrow-boats where the canal changed direction towards Hollinwood. Ignore this change in direction to keep straight on up the slope to reach the Fairbottom Branch of the canal.

Turn right on this branch's towpath towards the Pennines, with Hartshead Pike's tower clearly visible ahead. The canal here is filled with a fine display of rushes with only occasional edging stones as evidence of its former existence. The broad smooth towpath makes for easy walking (but also high speeds from mountain bikers) and can be quite busy on summer weekends. After 600 metres, the canal narrows for a small aqueduct (this is over the lane used for alternative C – see map). Now ugly fencing mars the next stretch until the canal is in water once more, which lasts until just before the A627. The path uses a culvert along the line of the canal itself to pass under the road. Not surprisingly this can be very muddy, and the mud can continue as far as the end of the canal at Fennyfield Bridge. The drier alternative would be to leave the canal, turning left onto the A627 to the Park Bridge access road.

The road can in fact be followed all the way back to the start at Park Bridge (this was the route of the tramway from the canal to the works), but the recommended finish is to cross the road just before the bridge to a stile by a seat. Go over the stile and up a steep path (with steps) to a narrow lane. Turn right on this then in 40 metres right again on a path which gently descends the hillside past seats. Ignore a stile with a "Oldham Way" marker on the left and continue towards woodland. Keep generally straight on to cross a tiny stream by an overgrown wall, and pass several fenced-off mine shafts to the right. The path climbs again towards the edge of the valley as Park Bridge comes into view below on the right, the two ends of the embankment for the former viaduct (demolished in 1970) clearly visible. Keep on the path above a side valley, before descending steeply to a tiny footbridge and up steps to cross the railway embankment. It is worth turning right on this for 50 metres to the remains of a seat overlooking a splendid view of Park Bridge. Go back along the embankment, then turn right down a steep (stepped) path to pass below the wall of the Upper Roller Shed, with the landscaped remains of a cotton mill on the right, to the road just below the Visitor Centre and car park.

24. Another loop, another canal

Mossley

Use of this walk's railway as a transport link has gone for ever, unlike the nearby canal which, despite closing earlier than the railway, is now being brought back to "life".

Start: Mossley, on the A635 Manchester-Barnsley road, 2 miles north of Stalybridge. GR 974020.

Distance: 5km (just over 3 miles) with long level stretches, but also climbs at the end of both railway and canal sections.

Map: Pathfinder 713 "Oldham".

By car: Approaching Mossley from Stalybridge on the A635, turn right into Waggon Road just as housing begins on the **left**-hand side of the main road. There is limited parking on the left of Waggon Road -see inset map.

By public transport: Mossley station has trains on the Manchester-Wakefield service, plus regular buses from Manchester and Ashton-under-Lyne in particular (alight on the main road close to the station).

The LNWR line from Manchester to Leeds was opened through Standedge Tunnel in 1849 alongside the Huddersfield Narrow Canal whose tunnel had been completed 38 years earlier. The rail tunnel was for a single line, and a second single-line bore was added in 1871. Later the LNWR decided to raise the whole Manchester-Leeds line to four tracks. (A new double-track tunnel at Standedge was opened in 1894 which is the one in use today). As part of this, a new double-track loop was built on the **east** side of the Tame valley between Stalybridge and Diggle – the Micklehurst Loop. Goods traffic began on the loop in 1885, and passenger trains a year later, serving stations at Staley and Middlebrook, Micklehurst, Friezland and Uppermill. Local passenger traffic did not last long, Micklehurst closing as early as 1907, Staley and Middlebrook two years later, and Friezland and Uppermill completing the station closures in 1917.

The line continued to be busy with through trains and local goods traffic up to closure of the line in 1964, although goods services continued from Stalybridge to Friezland for another few months and to Millbrook power station until 1975. The section walked here is the most intact part of the rail route though it is possible to walk onwards, despite landscaping and some buildings over the actual route, through Greenfield and Uppermill to the former Butterhouse tunnel, south of Diggle.

The stretch of the Huddersfield Narrow Canal walked here was open for traffic by 1799 (although the whole canal did not come into use until the opening of the Standedge Tunnel in 1811). The LNWR lines soon removed most of its traffic, although some use lingered on till 1944 when the canal was abandoned. That appeared to be the end of the story, but in 1974 the Huddersfield Canal Society was formed with the aim of restoring the canal to use. Progress was slow for many years, but by 1998 over three-quarters of its length had been re-opened and the remaining 20 blockages should be removed by the end of the year 2000. This will once again allow boats to travel from the Ashton and Peak Forest canals at Ashton-under-Lyne to the Broad Canal at Huddersfield, through the historic Standedge Tunnel.

The Walk

From the car parking spaces, walk down Waggon Road (those using public transport could join this using Mill Street – see inset map). Follow the road as it swings right and crosses both river and canal. Keep on past the New Bridge public house – hereabouts the "loop" railway was carried over the road on the Mossley viaduct, demolished 1975-6. Turn left after the pub into Station Road, where in 100 metres on the left is the former Micklehurst station building, now well-restored as a private residence. The railway itself is reached by going left behind the building, at the "Tame Valley" sign. Go through gates to reach the trackbed at the northern end of the former viaduct, and continue along it, at first alongside the road, then curving right into a cutting and under a blackened brick bridge. Continue through the cutting, well-covered with heather on both sides, until the

The Micklehurst Loop was much used by goods traffic to relieve the original line on the other side of the Tame Valley, up to closure as a through route in 1964. *(J. Davenport)*

slopes ease and there are views out left over the Tame valley (though these are rapidly being obscured by fast-growing trees). The trackbed soon becomes hemmed in by woodland with views restricted to the hill ahead, overlooking Greenfield. The route bends gently left, through a gateway, then right, before coming to an end with a short sharp climb up to a road (here the railway used a tunnel which has been filled in).

Go through the gates onto the road and turn left towards the junction with the A635. Turn left here too, by the Royal George pub, and follow the A-road for 150 metres until it begins to bend left, just past signs for "Tameside/Mossley". Now head right at the wooden footpath sign for "Quick". (Do **not** take the path sign-posted "Public Footpath to Royal George Mills".) Follow the track down to the canal at another wooden signpost. The direction required is marked

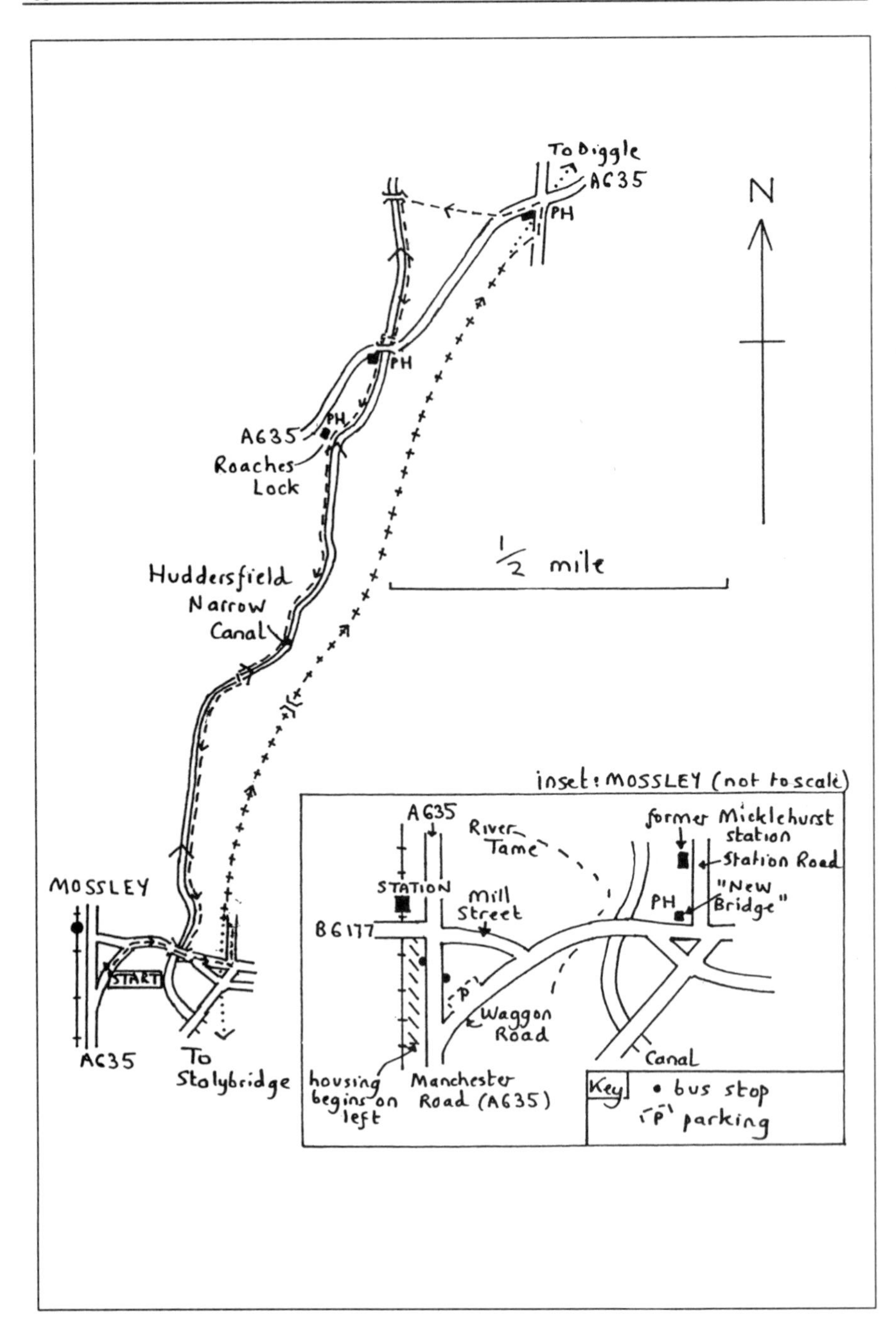
To Diggle
A635
PH
N
PH
PH
A635
Roaches Lock
½ mile
Huddersfield Narrow Canal
MOSSLEY
START
A635
To Stalybridge
inset: MOSSLEY (not to scale)
A635
River Tame
former Micklehurst station
Station Road
STATION
Mill Street
B6177
PH
"New Bridge"
P
Waggon Road
Canal
housing begins on left
Manchester Road (A635)
Key
• bus stop
P parking

"Scout Green 1¾ ml", but to gain this, take the path down to the right of the bridge, then left on the towpath back under the bridge. The towpath soon gives fine views over the Tame valley, before reaching the first of the four locks encountered on this section, with its typical pattern of a single gate at the uphill end but twin gates downhill. Next the canal swings right below modern stone-built houses to reach a second lock. Just past this, the towpath crosses over the canal, then goes under a road bridge and passes steps up to the Tollemarche Arms pub. Now despite a derelict mill on the left and factory units to the right, the canal enters quite a rural stretch, overhung by trees, before reaching Roaches Lock. The picnic site here is a pleasant spot, with views over the lock and its adjacent pub, and across the weir on the Tame to the present-day rail line on the hillside above.

Next is a broad stretch of canal, reed-fringed at the left, before it swings left, right and left again alongside the river. A further sharp right bend leads past the imposing remnants of Woodend Mill, downstream of a weir, to another lock. Immediately after this the towpath crosses back to the left-hand side of the canal, which now bends left past a cleared area of former mills on the far bank. A straight stretch of canal now leads to the final lock on this walk, followed by a curve round disused mills to the road bridge crossed on the outward journey. Go under this, then immediately left alongside railings to reach the road, where a left turn leads back across the canal and river towards the starting points.

25. On the trail of the "Donkey"

Delph

Almost the whole length of the former Delph branch is included on this walk, along with an historic stretch of the Huddersfield Narrow Canal and a visit to the attractive village of Dobcross.

Start: Wool Road car park, off the A670 just north of Uppermill (Saddleworth). GR 995065.

Distance: 5.75km (over 3½ miles) with 57 metres (185 ft) of ascent, mostly on one steep climb to Dobcross village.

Map: Pathfinder 713 "Oldham".

By car: Coming from the Manchester direction, the car park entrance is on the left, 250 metres north of the junction of the A670 with the A6052 from Delph and Denshaw. Coming from the other direction, it is on the right 150 metres after the Navigation pub.

By public transport: The nearest bus stops are on the A670 by the Navigation pub for services from Ashton-under-Lyne, and on the A6052 just before its junction with the A670 for services from Oldham.

The "Delph Donkey" was the name given to services on the Delph line, supposedly after the first means of traction after the branch was opened by the LNWR from Greenfield in 1851. Once Greenfield was connected to Oldham through Lydgate tunnel, Grotton and Lees, most trains operated on Oldham-Greenfield-Delph services. Passenger trains on the whole line ceased in 1955 and goods services to Delph ended eight years later. On the Delph branch itself, the only station at the start was at Delph, or more correctly New Delph (nearly half a mile from the village). Halts were added later at Moorgate, actually on the Manchester-Huddersfield main line, and Dobcross in 1912, and Measurements (named after the nearby mill) in 1932. Almost all the former branch is walkable (at least once away from the main line) apart from the final 200 metres into New Delph.

The history and redevelopment of the Huddersfield Narrow Canal are dealt with in walk 24. However the 500 metres stretch walked here is of great significance. Wool Road marked the limit of the canal west of the Pennines in the period 1799-1811, before the completion of Standedge Tunnel. Goods were thus unloaded here and sent on by pack-horse over the summit. A large warehouse and canal basin at Wool Road have been lost, but a smaller transhipment shed survives and has been restored by the canal society. The A670 next to this shed was one of the 20 blockages remaining in 1998. Here in the 1960s, a lock was infilled, the road realigned and the canal reduced to a pipe under the A670. As the next similar blockage was almost a mile away, the intervening stretch of canal was used by the society to promote the restoration project, with boat trips from the museum at Uppermill through two locks to Wool Road. This section was refurbished in the winter of 1998/9, with work on the restored link to the rest of the canal at Wool Road scheduled for 1999.

This 1956 railtour visit, seen here near Dobcross, was described in a local newspaper as "a bizarre trainload of antiquarians"! *(J. Davenport)*

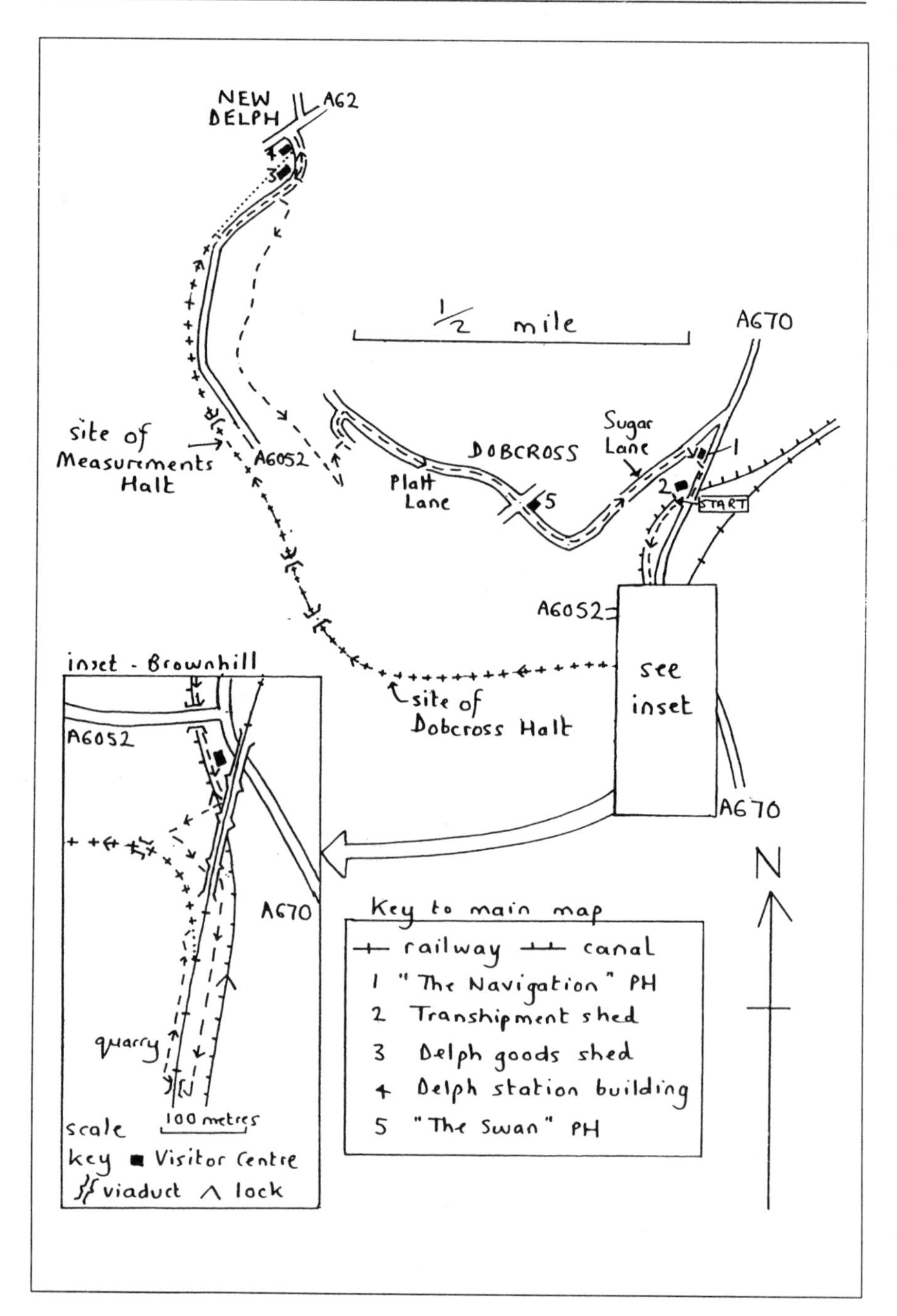

NEW DELPH
A62
1/2 mile
A670
site of Measurements Halt
A6052
DOBCROSS
Sugar Lane
Platt Lane
START
A6052
see inset
site of Dobcross Halt
A670
inset - Brownhill
A6052
A670
quarry
scale
100 metres
key ■ Visitor Centre
viaduct ∧ lock
N
Key to main map
railway canal
1 "The Navigation" PH
2 Transhipment shed
3 Delph goods shed
4 Delph station building
5 "The Swan" PH

The Walk

From the car park, first walk to the canal towpath to view the well-restored transhipment shed. Then return across the car park to its far end to join the towpath as it goes under the bridge carrying the A6052 and past the Brownhill Visitor Centre where displays, leaflets etc are housed in a 1916 highways depot! (This section of the walk is shown on the inset map.) Next is Limekiln Lock, almost under the magnificent railway viaduct carrying the Manchester-Leeds main line over the A670, the canal and the River Tame. Cross the canal by the footbridge at the far end of the lock (sign-posted "Clough Bottom Nurseries"), and go up the track. To the right are the scanty remains of Mytholm Mill, a late 18th-century fulling mill, though these do include the water-wheel pit. The track passes garages on the left to reach a tarmac lane. The bridge carrying the former Delph branch can be seen ahead, and the "official" walkable line starts there.

For the full route however turn left on the tarmac lane. This soon leads under the railway viaduct and swings right to run between canal and railway. Keep on the tarmac (Den Lane) for 250 metres after the viaduct. Here a clear path comes in from the right. Head up this path as it climbs (stonily) under the railway and becomes a narrow path alongside a wall heading back towards Brownhill. As the wall ends, another path is joined at a quarry entrance (this was Ladcastle quarry which once had its own siding from the branch). This path runs more visibly alongside the railway, which along this stretch used to have a separate line for the Delph branch. Soon bushes on the right indicate where the branch began to swing away from the route of the main line. As the path rounds a craggy spur on the left, it drops down right to join the former trackbed. Continue along the path as the line swings left beneath the gable end of a stone cottage, with views right over the valley and viaduct. The path crosses over the bridge seen previously and joins the "official" Delph Donkey track at a picnic table and gateway.

Now the broad former trackbed continues clearly ahead, with a garden centre below on the right, and Dobcross with its Italianate church visible across the valley. Pass beneath a fine stone cottage on the left – this is Mow Halls, an 18th-century clothier's house. Next the route bends right and crosses over Ladcastle Road. Here was Dobcross Halt, indicated by the recessed wall on the left just after the bridge. The trackbed continues to swing right, passing a picnic table and crossing first a stream, then a lane between two gateways. Next two bridges cross the track, the first wide enough to be a short tunnel, before reaching a gateway and a sign "Tame Valley Delph Donkey", at a point where views of a small valley open up on the left. This is the site of Measurements Halt, and is the furthest point of the "official" use of the former railway line, and the last point of easy exit to the A6052 on the right. The rail route is however still passable for another 600 metres, although after the next bridge it becomes a narrow path through an otherwise overgrown trackbed. This ends abruptly at an obstacle with no clear descent to the A-road below. However by retracing the route for about 30 metres back from the obstacle, a feasible path down to the road is reached. Take care on the last paces to the busy road, as the safety of the pavement is on the far side!

It is worth walking up the A-road to the junction at New Delph, to view the former station. First seen is the goods shed, still used for industrial purposes, then the station building, now a residence. Further along the platform is a rusting passenger coach, all that appears to remain of a collection that around 1980 also included a saddle tank loco, a brake van and an oil tank wagon. From the junction, walk back along the A6052 to just past the goods shed, where at a modern factory unit, a sign for "Gatehead ¼ ml" points left. Follow this path over the river on a footbridge to a T-junction of paths. Take the right-hand path as it follows the edge of the valley floor (some muddy patches are likely here) and goes beside a fenced-off pond and factory with metal chimneys and storage tank. Past these, the scenery improves as the path climbs above streams on the right and out onto an open slope with views across the valley. Keep on this clear path along the valley side as it descends and climbs rough steps above the river on the right.

Eventually the path meets another coming down the hillside from the left, at yellow marker signs. Turn back left here uphill until the path forks at a fence line running downhill. Take the right fork as it climbs steeply up between garden fences to reach a road with modern houses (Bar Meadow). Turn left here and follow the road as it swings right to meet a "main" road (Platt Lane). Turn right and pass more modern housing to Platt Lane Farm (right) and the former school (left). Now the housing is older as the road leads to the centre of Dobcross – the Square. This makes a most attractive stopping point, with the Swan pub (1765) ahead, Lane End House (1780) on the left, and the former Saddleworth Bank to the right among its historic buildings.

Carry approximately straight on, with the Swan on the left, into Sugar Lane. This soon swings left to give views ahead up the Tame valley to the Diggle flight of locks on the canal. As the road descends with the fine conversion of Stonebottom Mill to residences on the right, there are also views back down valley to the railway viaduct, with the route of the Delph branch cut into the hillside on its right. Just before the first buildings on the right, a path descends steeply to the A670 by the Navigation pub, where a right turn on the A-road leads back to the car park.

Bibliography and Further Reading

Two books have been essential sources for the railway history of these walks:

"The North West" Volume 10 in the "Regional History of the Railways of Great Britain" series. This was originally written by Geoffrey Holt and published in 1978. The version used here was a second edition, revised by Gordon Biddle and published in 1986. (Both versions were published by David and Charles.)

"North-West England" by John Marshall, in the "Forgotten Railways" series, published by David and Charles in 1981.

Also invaluable for the industrial background to many of the walks was:

"The Industrial Archaeology of Lancashire" by Owen Ashmore. This was published in 1969 by David and Charles in the "Industrial Archaeology of the British Isles" series.

Note that in the "Gazetteer" section of the last two books, features are described as they were 20-30 years ago, but these are not necessarily still in place.

Not specifically about railways but providing much general information in the area of Walks 8-9 and 11-13 are:

"Rossendale Rambles" and "Further Rossendale Rambles" by Ian Goldthorpe (Rossendale Groundwork Trust 1985 and 1991).

Similarly, Glasson Dock (Walk 2), Haigh Hall estate (15) and Pennington Flash (16) are in:

"Field Excursions: North West England" (ed. C. Park, University of Lancaster/Cicerone Press, 1990).

Books about specific **railways** (their companies, lines and branches) are plentiful. Two particularly useful sources, as they covered more than one walk, were:

"Railways and Mineral Tramways of Rossendale" by B. Roberts (Oakwood Press 1974) for Walks 11-13, and

"The East Lancashire Railway" by R.W. Rush (Oakwood Press 1983) for Walks 4 and 7-12.

There are many more readily available books which are largely collections of photographs but do include some text, for example "The Lancashire and Yorkshire Railway – Then and Now" by A.

Earnshaw (Ian Allan, 1992). On a more detailed level, the industries and their railways in the area of Walks 15-21 are comprehensively covered in the series on the industrial railways of the Wigan Coalfield/Bolton, Bury and Manchester Coalfield by C. H. A. Townley et al. (Runpast Publishing 1991-5).

Finally, there are numerous leaflets available from Tourist Information Centres and libraries in the areas concerned. The most useful of these are credited in the text but special mention must be made of the excellent leaflets produced by the City of Salford (Walks 19 and 20).

Also of interest:

ARCHAEOLOGY WALKS IN THE PEAK DISTRICT

Ali Cooper

These walks explore archaeological sites where there are visible pre-historic features in the landscape: Bronze age barrows, stone circles, caves, mines and much more. Walks are from 3 to 12 miles and are fully illustrated. The book includes an introduction to the study of archaeology and a glossary of the terminology used. Brief descriptions of the major finds on the walks are included, plus a bibliography for those who wish to delve deeper. Ali Cooper has an MA in archeaology and is a keen outdoors enthusiast.
£7.95

DISCOVERY WALKS IN LANCASHIRE

Brian Conduit

This new 'Discovery Walks' guide contains 30 routes of assorted lengths suitable for hardy walkers and casual family strollers. All walks have a heritage theme and enable you to appreciate both Lancashire's rich historical legacy as well as its ever-changing landscape. The walks visit Roman remains, medieval castles and abbeys, nature reserves, country parks and many monuments to the country's role in the industrial revolution.
All the walks contain information on types of terrain, distance and degree of difficulty, refreshments and public transport. To add to the variety, three urban walks in Lancaster, Liverpool and Manchester are included. *£6.95*

WEST PENNINE WALKS

Mike Cresswell

Bolton's Mike Cresswell is renowned for the accuracy of his instructions and his impish humour. In this second edition he has re-walked every single one of his routes exploring the countryside of the delightful West Pennine area. *£7.95*

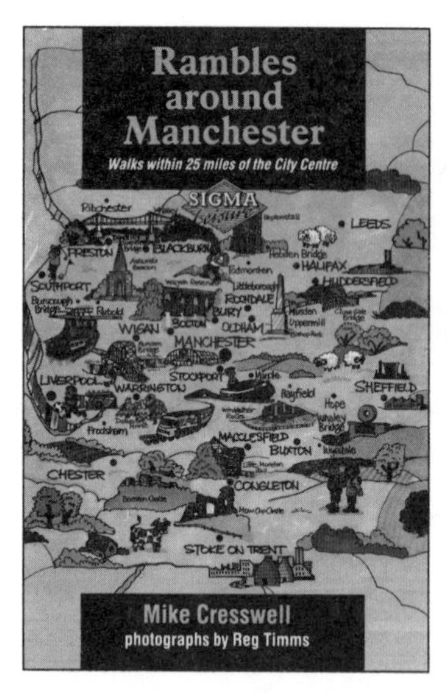

RAMBLES AROUND MANCHESTER

Mike Cresswell

Take the bus or train from the city centre and discover the treats around Manchester. "Written with fun, rare talent and impish humour" BOLTON EVENING NEWS. *£5.95*

BEST TEA SHOP WALKS IN LANCASHIRE

Clive Price

Walk through breathtaking upland scenery, lush river valleys and along impressive coastal paths and complete your day by indulging in the celebrated English pastime of afternoon tea.This "refreshing blend of walks and tea shops which reveals the.. delights of the Lancashire countryside and culinary arts" helps you get the very best out of Lancashire. *£6.95*

BEST PUB WALKS IN LANCASHIRE

Neil Coates

Lancashire has a rich pub heritage and a surprising variety of countryside for invigorating walks. This is the most comprehensive guidebook of its type. *£6.95*

50 CLASSIC WALKS IN LANCASHIRE

Terry Marsh

This sequel to "50 Classic Walks in the Pennines" takes walkers through the much neglected, and far-reaching, county of Lancashire. There are many fine expanses of good walking country and places of beauty within the county's boundaries - known to the locals but waiting to be discovered by the wider population. With a map to accompany each walk, his own photographs and a comprehensive index, Terry Marsh again shares his vast experience. *£7.95*

WEST LANCASHIRE WALKS

Michael Smout

No need to venture into touristy areas, it's all on the doorstep for Lancashire's walkers - "Knowledgeable guide to 25 rambles by the Ramblers' West Lancs Group Chairman" RAMBLING TODAY. *£6.95*

EAST LANCASHIRE WALKS

Michael Smout

The rambling reverend continues his revelation! This companion volume to "West Lancashire Walks" leads you to an abundance of walking and places of interest which lie just beyond your urban doorstep to the East - a haunted house near Warrington, an American Wood at Aspel, there's even a giant on the banks of the Mersey! *£5.95*

WALKING IN EDEN

Ron Scholes

Walk through Eden's light limestone landscape, view its red sandstone gorge and woodland scenery, and you'll feel as if surrounded by a secluded northern paradise. Ron Scholes guides you through this forgotten wilderness in his 30 circular and direct walks which illustrate the rich variety of walking in Eden. *£6.95*

WALKS IN MYSTERIOUS LANCASHIRE

Graham Dugdale

Delving into a host of mysterious places throughout Lancashire, this unusual collection of 30 walks, suitable for all the family, will appeal to walkers with enquiring minds. From the enchanting follies of Lord Levenshulme of Bivington to the origins of the 'American Dream' in Worton, history and legend are inextricably linked in this succession of fine walks set in the superb Lancashire landscape. Lucid walking directions and the author's ornate, hand-drawn maps complement the entertaining commentary. *£6.95*

TOWNS & VILLAGES OF BRITAIN: LANCASHIRE

Michael Smout

Full of historical facts and liberally laced with tales of hauntings, witchery and enchantment - the moors, valleys and mossland of Lancashire are the backdrop to this new, comprehensive gazetteer of the county's towns and villages. Michael Smout is keen to emphasise that Lancashire's austere, industrial mill towns often obscure a rich, varied, often eerie past. Pendle, in the depths of central Lancashire, is witch country, Claughton bears the story of the house that moved, whilst Chingle Hall near Goosenargh is reputedly the most haunted in the country. "The histories of our towns and villages neatly gathered in one definitive guide" SOUTHPORT VISITER *£8.95*

BY-WAY BIKING IN LANCASHIRE

Henry Tindell

From Morecambe Bay to Bolton and from Blackpool to Burnley, Henry Tindell reveals Lancashire's outstanding potential as a destination for mountain bikers. 27 routes explore a fine variety of off-road tracks which lead you to a wealth of countryside and villages all within easy reach of the large northern towns and cities. As well as routes for the hardened off-roader, Henry has included some safe riding and easy trails suitable for the young and old.
£7.95

All of our books are available from your local bookshop. In case of difficulty, or to obtain our complete catalogue, contact:

Sigma Leisure, 1 South Oak Lane,
Wilmslow, Cheshire SK9 6AR
Phone: 01625-531035. Fax: 01625-536800.
E-mail: info@sigmapress.co.uk

http://www.sigmapress.co.uk

MASTERCARD and VISA welcome.